THIS IS
Sailing

D0675796

Fourth Edition

THIS IS
Sailing
A COMPLETE COURSE

**Edited by
Jim Saltonstall**

Adlard Coles Nautical

London

BRIDGWATER COLLEGE

797.124 SAL

BO123969

Cypher	25.12.04
	£15.99

This edition published 2002 by Adlard Coles Nautical
an imprint of A&C Black (Publishers) Ltd
37 Soho Square, London W1D 3QZ
www.adlardcoles.co.uk

Copyright © Delius Klasing & Co 1996

First edition 1973
Reprinted 1973, 1974, 1975, 1977, 1979, 1981
Second edition 1984
Reprinted 1984, 1985
Third edition 1991
Reprinted 1992, 1995
Fourth edition 1996
Paperback edition 2002

ISBN 0-7136-6359-6

All rights reserved. No part of this publication
may be reproduced in any form or by any means –
graphic, electronic or mechanical, including
photocopying, recording, taping or information
storage and retrieval systems – without the prior
permission in writing of the publishers.

A CIP catalogue record for this book is available
from the British Library.

Note: While all reasonable care has been taken in
the publication of this book, the publisher takes
no responsibility for the use of the methods or
products described in the book.

A&C Black uses paper produced with elemental
chlorine-free pulp, harvested from managed
sustainable forests.

Typeset in 10 on 11H pt Sabon by
Falcon Oast Graphic Art Ltd
Printed and bound in Italy

Contents

Preface

Sailing is one of the most popular participation sports and attracts many newcomers each year. At a recent Sailing Coach Conference, a sports psychologist was quoted as saying: 'Sailing is the most challenging of all sports because it has so many variables to consider'. How true that quotation is. No two days' sailing are ever the same; there are always new challenges to overcome and new skills to learn. I first discovered this many years ago whilst I was crewing on *HMS Victory*; now, as British Olympic Team Coach, I am still learning about the sport.

Continuously in print since 1973, *This is Sailing* has introduced thousands of new sailors to the sport. I was very pleased to be asked to act as consultant editor on this new edition which has been thoroughly revised and updated. Following the style and content of the previous editions, the text and illustrations are laid out in spread-by-spread, easy to follow modules, covering all the important practical topics: from rigging the boat and launching, through to recovery and towing. Essential sailing manoeuvres such as tacking, gybing and how to handle a capsize are also well covered.

With the aid of new, carefully-planned photo sequences and artwork, *This is Sailing* will give you a good working knowledge of the theory of sailing so that when you set sail with friends or start a sailing course, you will know what to expect; some basic knowledge will give you confidence and enable you to learn quicker. Also it is very reassuring to have a reference book at home to refer to after a days' sailing when your head is spinning with terms and manoeuvres and you want to quietly review what you have learned.

You can dip into the sections on handling techniques for both helm and crew and brush up on the theory of wind to understand boat balance and trim better. Later, as you gain experience, the sections on basic spinnaker work and trapezing will give you a useful grounding.

Although we are concentrating on the theory of dinghy sailing for the beginner here, you will find that once you have mastered the basics, the principles are the same for any kind of sailing, whatever size and type of boat.

Always remember though, that the sea is its own master and commands respect. If you ensure that your early sailing experiences are in controlled and friendly conditions, where you feel safe and comfortable, you will really enjoy yourself in your earliest stages of learning and will look forward keenly to the challenges of the sport.

Sailing techniques

Running before the wind

Dinghy running before the wind. Mainsail and jib are set on different sides (goosewinged). The crew sit on opposite sides to balance the boat

Sailing with the wind coming from behind, from *astern*, is the most basic form of sailing. The first sailing boats were just pushed along by the wind. The more resistance you offered to the wind, in the form of more sail area, the faster you were pushed along.

In the case of modern sailing boats, that means arranging the sails in such a way that as large an area as possible is presented to the wind. Whilst keeping control of the boat, the sails are set as nearly as possible at right-angles to the wind, with the sheets eased right off. Since the jib is hidden from the wind by the mainsail if both sails are on the same side and it cannot catch the wind, it is *goosewinged* (taken across to the opposite side).

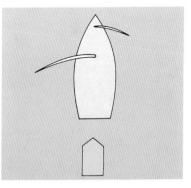

Above: running before the wind with spinnaker set. There is more life in the boat. Things can become difficult if the wind picks up

Right: sailing with the wind not quite astern, as can be seen by the flag on the buoy. The sails are both set on the same side

The helmsman and crew distribute their weight evenly between the two sides. Care must be taken, however, because the sail area is divided unequally between the sides. If you let go of the tiller, you will find that the boat begins to turn of its own accord because the power of the large mainsail is greater than that of the jib. So the boat will turn away from the side with the mainsail. This is called luffing which could lead to *broaching*. To gain more speed when running before the wind you can hoist extra sail area in the form of a spinnaker. But beware; this parachute-shaped sail is harder to control than the other two. It can destabilize the boat so steering becomes difficult and it begins to roll from side to side. Fortunately, this only tends to happen in stronger winds, but in those conditions it is wiser not to hoist the spinnaker.

Broad reaching

If the wind is neither astern (coming from behind) nor on the beam (blowing at right-angles to the way you are going), but coming from somewhere in between the two, then the boat is said to be sailing

Helmsman and crew sit on opposite sides on a broad reach to balance the boat. Although the helmsman may sit on the leeward side, as here, it is generally easier to steer from the other side

Left: for a broad reach both sails are let out at a wide angle to the boat

Below: from out on the trapeze the crew has a good view of the spinnaker which she is controlling

on a broad reach. Both sails are set on the leeward side of the boat (the side farthest from the wind) and the sheets are eased well out. To trim the sails the helm and crew sit either on opposite sides or both on the windward side (the side nearest the wind), depending on the strength of the wind. The spinnaker can also be used on a broad reach, if the wind is not too strong, to give the boat considerably more speed. If there is a lot of wind, the crew may get out on the trapeze to keep the boat sailing reasonably upright. Since the wind does not push the boat sideways too much when running before the wind or broad-reaching, the centreboard can be raised two thirds of the way up. The sails are no longer set at a 90° angle to the wind direction, but sheeted in a little more. This means the wind is not just striking the sails at right-angles, as on a run, but is deflected slightly by the sails and actually flows round them. This makes the boat go faster; a broad reach with spinnaker set is a very fast course relative to the wind.

13

Bearing away

The dinghy is sailing on a broad reach in a light wind, with sheets eased slightly

The helmsman pulls the tiller towards him and lets out the mainsail

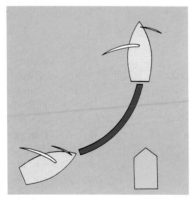

Bearing away means altering course so that the boat turns *away* from the wind. As it turns, the angle at which it meets the wind also changes, so the sails need to be adjusted progressively to suit the new situation. Since the wind is coming more and more from behind, the sheets are eased little by little, to maintain the right trim of the sails.

During the turn, the boat has less and less tendency to lean over because the force of the wind is increasingly from behind rather than from the side. Helmsman and crew therefore redistribute their weight to maintain the boat's upright position.

In fact, whenever you change course towards a point further to leeward you will always be bearing away. Often, bearing away is done in preparation for a gybe (see page 34). As the wind comes astern, the jib can be taken across to the opposite side to the main.

The boat comes more upright. The crew redistribute their weight across the boat

The wind is not yet dead astern. The helmsman continues to bear away

The boat is running before the wind. The jib can now be taken across to the starboard side

As can be seen from the wake it has left behind in the water, the dinghy has come up from the bottom right-hand corner of the photograph. Now it is bearing away after rounding the buoy. In the process both sheets must be eased

15

Luffing on to a beam reach

To luff means to alter course *towards* the direction from which the wind is coming. So the tiller is moved towards the side where the mainsail is. It makes no difference whether the boat turns to port or to starboard; you are always luffing if you turn towards the wind.

In our example, the boat is sailing with the wind coming from astern (running before the wind). The two sails are set on opposite sides. The windward side is taken to be the side opposite the mainsail. In this case, windward is port (the left side of the boat, looking ahead).

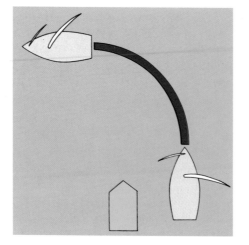

The course sailed by the boat as it turns, viewed from above

⑤

The helmsman pulls the tiller towards the mainsail. The boat turns to port; it luffs. This means that the jib must be taken across to starboard, because the wind is coming more and more from the port side. The helmsman, too, should move across and sit to windward, to counteract the increasing tendency of the boat to lean to one side (to heel) under the pressure of the wind which is now coming from the port side. At the same time, both sails must be trimmed in more tightly, until they just stop fluttering, but no more. The boat is sailing on a beam reach when the wind is at right-angles to the direction in which the boat is travelling. If the wind is light the boat should be allowed to heel a little to leeward, so that gravity helps the sails to adopt the correct angle and curvature.

1 Sailing with wind astern, sails on opposite sides

2 The tiller is pulled towards the mainsail

3 The wind is now coming over the port side. The jib is sheeted in on the other side

4 The helmsman moves over to the windward side

5 The boat is on a beam reach, with a slight heel

Luffing up to close-hauled

As we have said, luffing means turning the boat towards the wind. In other words, it is the opposite of bearing away. As with bearing away, it is not simply a matter of steering the boat round on to the new course; the sheets must be adjusted progressively during the turn, gradually pulling in the sails so that the boat does not slow down because the sails have begun to flap.

Usually the wind starts to heel the boat more so the weight of the crew is needed on the windward side, or even sitting out over the sidedeck, so that the boat is kept sailing moderately upright.

A boat will always be luffing when it turns further to windward than its previous course. As it turns the two sails are gradually sheeted in more tightly so that, on the one hand, they do not flap or flutter, but, on the other hand, they are not pulled in too tight. They should always be almost on the point of fluttering along the leading edge, so that they are using the wind as efficiently as possible. Only when the boat is close-hauled (sailing as close to the wind as possible) are the sheets pulled in fully.

1 **Reaching with sheets eased and centreboard half-raised**

2 **Preparing to luff. The centreboard can be lowered at this stage**

3 **Both sheets are pulled in steadily as the boat turns**

4 **As the boat luffs the crew may need to start sitting out**

5 **For sailing close-hauled the sails are sheeted in and the centreboard is down**

Windshifts when close-hauled

The wind that you actually experience on a boat is called the *apparent* wind. It is slightly different in strength and direction from the real (true) wind, because when the boat is moving it creates its own head wind. The apparent wind is a combination of that and the true wind.

If a gust comes the true wind suddenly gets stronger, while the speed of the boat responds less immediately and for a moment the head wind remains just as it was. This has the effect of momentarily changing the direction of the apparent wind, making it come more from the side. This fact can be exploited by the helmsman when beating as he can luff up, following the windshift round. Once the boat has gathered speed he will have to bear away again.

On the other hand, if the wind drops suddenly the boat's speed will be maintained for a few seconds and the apparent wind will come more from ahead. The sails will start to flutter and the boat has to bear away so the wind can fill them again.

1 **Sailing close-hauled, at as narrow an angle to the wind as possible**

2 **A gust comes. Luff up and take advantage of the windshift**

3 **The boat picks up speed, and the wind comes from further ahead. Bear away gradually**

4 **A sudden lull and the wind comes from right ahead. Bear away at once**

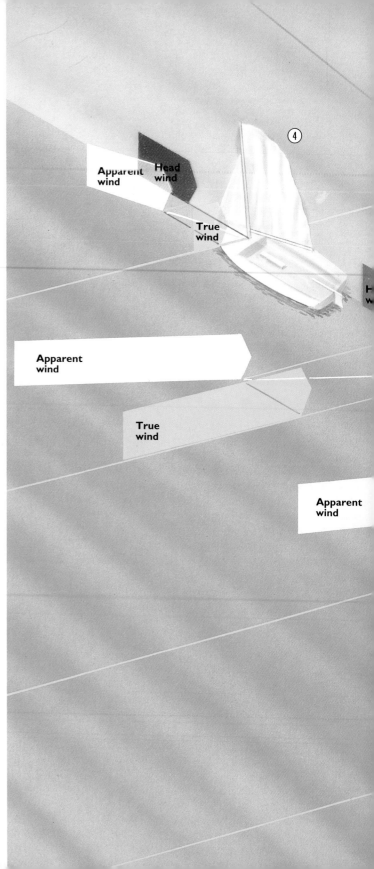

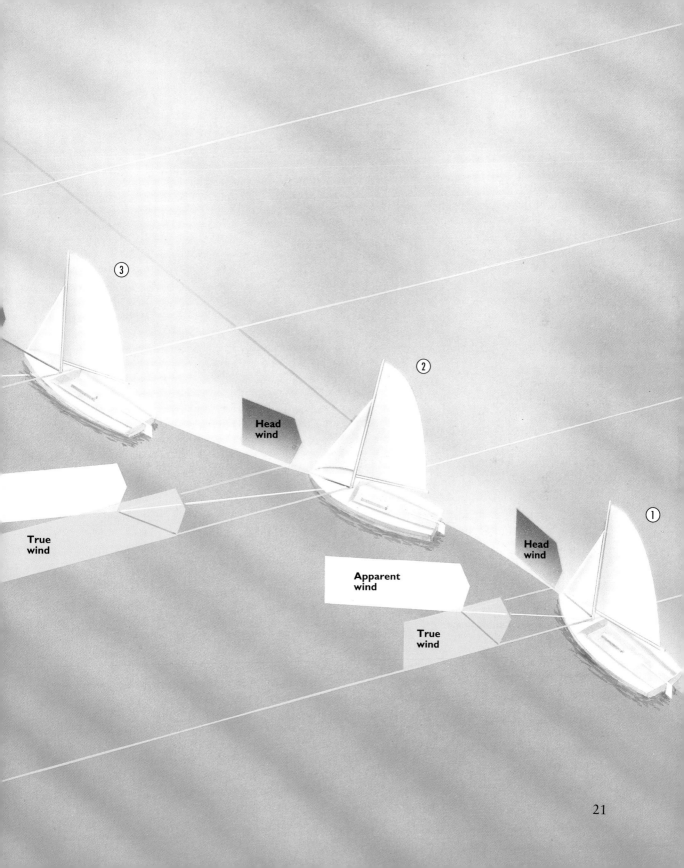

③

②

**Head
wind**

①

**Head
wind**

**True
wind**

**Apparent
wind**

**True
wind**

Beating to windward

You cannot sail straight into the wind. Instead, you must adopt a zigzag route, first sailing one way, then the other.

This is called *beating to windward*. The aim is to sail fast, without having to sail farther than necessary. In our illustration, the middle boat has found the best compromise. The other boats show that a shorter route leads to too much loss of speed, because the boat is heading too much into the wind to sail well (left), and that the route to be covered becomes too long if the boat does not point high enough into the wind, even if it is sailing faster (right).

It can be very difficult in practice to pick the best route to windward if windshifts caused by features on land, or clouds, also have to be taken into account. The trim and cut of the sails, the distribution of crew weight and constant attention to steering are all important for top performance. Skill in beating to windward is extremely important. Most sailing races begin with a beat and it is all too easy to get into the lee of competitors right at the start and fall back, blanketed by the leading boats.

When beating, the helmsman must always be trying to point as high as possible. At the same time, he should constantly compare his speed with that of other boats. Building up real skill in sailing to windward demands a good deal of 'feel' and experience.

Three boats beating to windward towards a jetty. The middle one gets there first. The left-hand boat has less far to sail, but goes too slowly; the right-hand boat sails faster, but has further to go

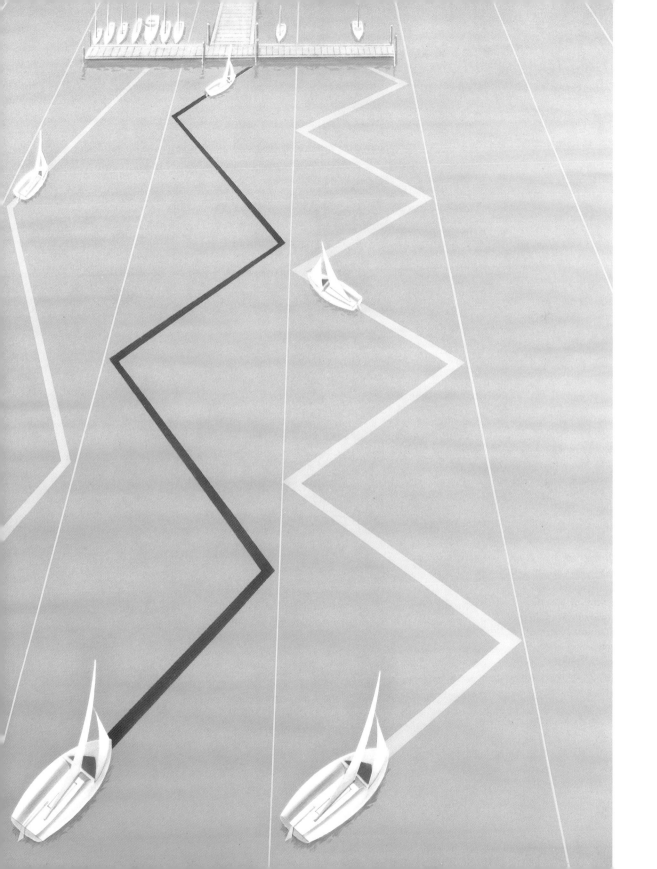

Tacking

1–2 Sailing close-hauled with the wind on the starboard side (starboard tack)

3 The tiller is pushed across. The boat comes upright and the sails start to flap

4 The jib is pulled across to starboard. Crew and sails change sides

5 The tack is complete and the sails fill once more on port tack

Tacking or *going about* is a change in course of about 90° during which the sails cross over to the other side. It involves turning through the sector in which it is impossible to sail because the wind is coming from dead ahead. As a result tacking involves a loss of speed. If the boat has not got enough speed beforehand to carry it through the turn, it will run out of steam and will not answer to the tiller. The tiller should not be turned too sharply either, because this too has a braking effect.

You tack at the end of each diagonal leg of a beating course. Both crew members change over to the opposite side.

Maintaining speed while tacking

Because the boat is constantly losing way (forward motion) while it is tacking, it is important to get the wind back in the sails as quickly as possible and regain speed. On the other hand, a rudder which is turned too much will act as a brake because the blade is at a sharp angle to the water flow. Consequently this will result in a loss of speed.

A compromise has to be found between this loss of speed and the time taken to complete the tack. If the tiller is not pushed far enough, there is a very long delay, with speed dropping all the time, until the wind catches the sails again on the new side. It usually turns out that the best rudder angle is about 33° to the centreline of the boat. That usually means, in practice, that the tiller should not be pushed beyond the side of the boat. This represents the best compromise between loss of speed and time taken to tack.

It is especially important not to come to a stop when tacking if the waves are short and steep, because a boat with no way on (which has lost all speed) cannot be steered.

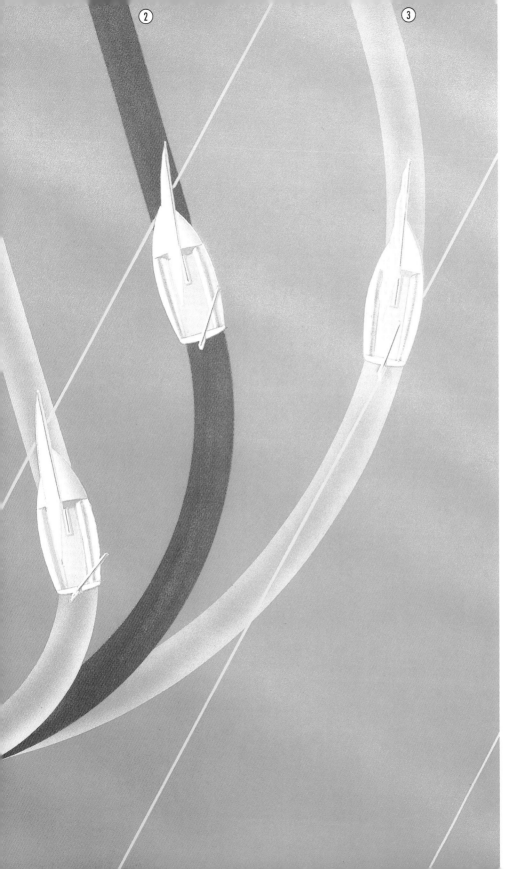

1 The tiller is too far over, resulting in a sharp turn and too much loss of speed while tacking

2 The right tiller angle, resulting in a smooth turn with minimal loss of speed

3 The tiller is not far enough over, resulting in a very gradual turn. It is not certain that the boat will get round at all before it comes to a complete halt

Wheelbarrow turn

Also called *wearing round*, this is a change of direction of more than 180° which includes tacking. The boat ends up by sailing across its own wake. It may be preferable to tack round in this way, instead of gybing, if a gybe seems too dangerous owing to the strength of wind. Nevertheless, this manoeuvre is not as easy as you might think at first, because the boat loses speed very quickly in just such conditions of strong wind and waves. So during the first phase you should not luff any more quickly than you can trim the sails to the new wind direction. The important thing is to have the boat sailing properly throughout, with the sails correctly trimmed, especially until you tack. A successful turn is the result of a series of separate operations. If you forget this you will come to a halt half-way round.

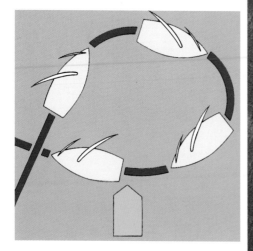

1 The dinghy sails up on a broad reach on starboard tack

2 The helmsman pushes the tiller to leeward and the sails are sheeted in progressively as the boat luffs

3 The boat is maintaining a good speed as it comes up to tacking

4 After tacking the wind fills the sails on the new side

5 The boat bears away and the sheets are let out progressively to suit the wind direction

6 The turn is complete. The boat sails across its own wake on port tack

29

Stopping

Left: the boat approaches the buoy on a beam reach. The helmsman judges the distance which the boat will need to come to a stop

Below: the helmsman luffs slightly to decrease the distance to the buoy

It is not easy to stop a sailing boat, at least not so as to come to rest at a specific place, like a jetty. The only way is to turn the boat directly into the wind to make it lose speed. This is known as luffing *head-to-wind*. Judgement is needed to gauge how far the boat will travel head-to-wind before it stops. It is easiest to start from a reaching course as, by luffing or bearing away slightly, you can put the boat in exactly the right place to begin the manoeuvre. Once you are downwind of your goal, the sheets are released and the helmsman puts the tiller hard over to turn into the wind.

As you gain experience of the basic procedure, you will soon be able to predict the distance which the boat will take to stop in different wind conditions.

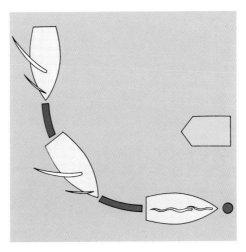

Below left: when the buoy is upwind the sheets are freed right off and the tiller put hard over. The boat shoots head-to-wind

Below right: with sails flapping, the boat slows to a halt exactly to leeward of the buoy

Windshifts when reaching

Even though a boat may be sailing in a straight line from one point to another, the strength and direction of the wind which it encounters will still vary. This means constantly trimming the sails to meet the changing wind direction.

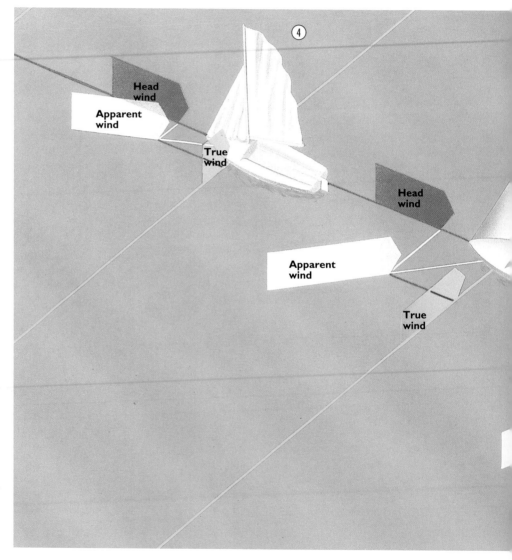

1 **Reaching with sails trimmed correctly**

2 **The true wind strengthens and the apparent wind comes more from the side. Ease the sheets slightly**

3 **The true wind lessens and the apparent wind shifts further ahead: sheet in**

4 **The true wind drops completely and the apparent wind shifts ahead: sheet in tight**

For example, a change in wind speed alone will alter the direction of the apparent wind. If the wind strengthens the boat does not respond instantaneously, but continues at the same speed. The head wind, therefore, remains the same. This means that the apparent wind comes from further abeam, a so-called *freeing* shift. The sheets can be eased by the corresponding amount. In the reverse case, if the wind drops, the apparent wind will suddenly come from further ahead (a *heading* shift). The crew must immediately react to this by sheeting the sails in more.

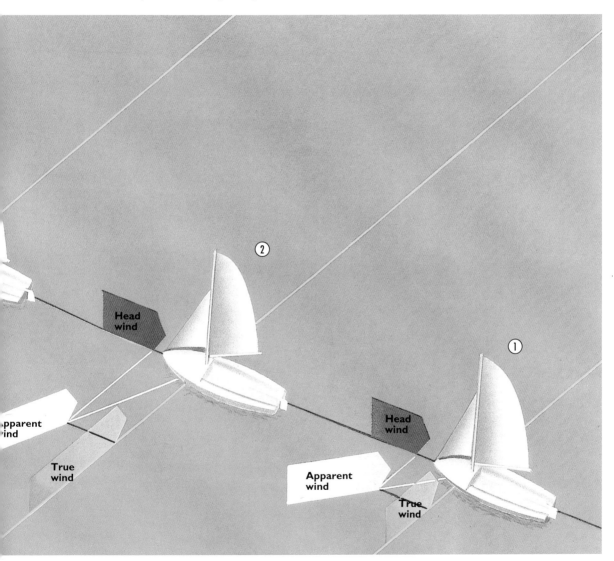

Gybing

1 **Preparing to go round the buoy, the boat approaches broad-reaching on starboard tack**

2 **The helmsman takes hold of the mainsheet ready to swing the boom across and pushes the tiller to windward. The crew ducks**

Gybing means that the sails change sides with the wind coming from astern. Unlike tacking, gybing happens quite suddenly and, at times, violently. If the crew are not ready for it, in a fresh wind it can result in a capsize.

The boom should not be left to swing across the boat of its own accord; the helmsman grabs the mainsheet about half-way along (or the crew grabs the kicking-strap) and at the right moment the boom is swung across under control.

At the same moment the windward side abruptly becomes the leeward side and the crew must move quickly to keep the boat in balance. Throughout the operation the helmsman must keep control of the boat's course.

3 The boom is swung across. The helmsman momentarily pulls the tiller back the other way, which helps keep the boat on an even keel

4 The helmsman lets go of the mainsheet. The crew adjusts the jib

5 The gybe complete, the boat is now broad-reaching on port tack

③ ④ ⑤

Heeling forces when gybing

(1)   (2)

As the boom swings across, several forces are acting on the boat (1), which could in an extreme case lead to a capsize. These forces include the weight of the crew, the pressure of the wind on the sails and centrifugal force. The last is aggravated by the boom swinging across and can be counteracted using the rudder. The boat tries to turn farther and the helmsman's job is to prevent this.

Helmsman and crew (or helmsman alone in a singlehanded boat like the one above) should make sure that they are sitting to windward immediately the boom goes across. This removes one of the three heeling forces (2). The next task is to minimize the centrifugal force. This can be achieved by ensuring that the boat is sailing straight ahead as the boom flies across and tries to impart a turning

motion to the boat. It is usually necessary to steer momentarily in the opposite direction (3). The final task is to ensure that the wind does not cause the boat to heel. If the mainsail is completely eased off, until it is almost at right-angles to the boat, the force of the wind will act forwards and not sideways (4).

One more tip. The centreboard should be raised halfway during the gybe, so that the boat cannot 'trip' over it after gybing and capsize as a result.

37

Coming to land

③

④

The operation of coming to land, ending with shooting head-to-wind, is viewed here from an upwind position. The dinghy approaches in a light wind, which

⑤

⑥

② ①

will, in fact, slow the boat down very little when it does head into the wind. The helmsman gauges the forward motion of the boat and the distance it can travel as it coasts in to the jetty. At this stage the painter (the line fastened to the bow) must be made ready to tie the boat up on arrival.

The end of the jetty is abeam. It is time to let fly the sheets and put the tiller hard over to make a sharp turn. The sails must be able to flap freely as soon as the turn is begun, so that the combination of wind pressure and centrifugal force does not cause the boat to heel.

In the final stage the boat coasts into the wind, sails flapping, until ideally it draws up close to the jetty and the crew can reach out to slow it to a stop. If it runs out of steam in the final approach, the whole procedure must be begun again.

But it is better to come to land safely at the second attempt than to arrive with a crash the first time around! This is especially true when sailing heavier boats, which are not as easy to fend off.

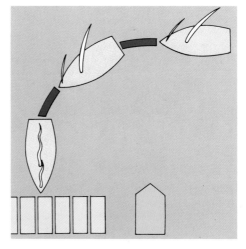

1 The dinghy approaches on a reach. The jetty lies to windward

2 The helmsman aims a bit to leeward of his goal. The amount depends on the speed of the boat

3 The boat arrives downwind of the jetty

4 The boat shoots into the wind with sails flapping

5 Its momentum carries it up to the jetty

6 The crew jumps ashore and holds on to the boat

39

The jib is backed on the windward side and the tiller is put over

The bow turns away from the wind

Getting under way

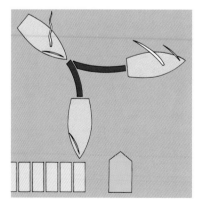

The sails are usually hoisted with the boat pointing head-to-wind. As a boat cannot sail straight into the wind, and it cannot be steered either until it is moving through the water, something will probably have to be done to get it moving, before you can start steering. If circumstances allow, a firm push forwards as the crew climbs into the boat may solve the problem.

However, this may not be possible, for example, if the boat is pointing towards a jetty, so another method must be used. The crew holds the jib out to the side. This is called *backing* the jib because the

The wind catches the mainsail. The jib is sheeted in on the leeward side and the tiller is centred

The boat has gathered speed and can be steered normally

wind catches it on the opposite side to normal. Now if you let go of the jetty the boat will start to move backwards, turning as it does so. You can help it along with the rudder, pointing it in the direction you want the stern (not the bow) to go.

Eventually the boat will have turned far enough to sail normally. This moment has come when the mainsail, sheeted in fairly tightly, ceases to flap and begins to draw (fill with wind). Then the jib can be sheeted in on the leeward side, so it is no longer backed. At this stage it is essential to centre the tiller, so that the boat can

gather speed. If you try to alter course too soon, before gathering speed, you will slow the boat down again. The rudder blade acts as a brake, as we have already mentioned. So centre the tiller, gather speed, and only then start to steer.

Backing the jib can be useful not only when setting off, but at any time when the boat has stopped head-to-wind. It is the best way of turning the boat away from the wind and getting it sailing again.

41

The mainsail is lowered and the boom is detached from the mast

When the boat is head-to-wind the crew starts lowering the mainsail

The helmsman starts to luff up into the wind while still some way off the beach

Landing on a beach with wind astern

If the wind is blowing towards the shore as you come to land, it is essential to approach the shore slowly. Since the wind is from astern it is not easy to reduce speed, short of towing a bucket behind the boat. This makes it important to lower the mainsail in good time. To do this, the boat is first turned head-to-wind. When the sails begin to flap the mainsail can be lowered. Care must be taken to prevent the boom crashing down on to the deck. Without the mainsail, the boat loses power, and the sail is arranged tidily to reduce wind resistance to a minimum.

Standing in the water, the crew guides the boat on to the sand

When the water is shallow enough the crew jumps out

With only the jib set, the helmsman steers for the beach

The mainsail is tidied out of the way so it does not catch the wind

The boat is now stationary and cannot be steered, so the jib is backed to blow the bow round and bring the wind round to the side and finally over the stern. If the boat is still going too fast, even under jib alone, then that too can be lowered or pulled in tight so that it cannot be filled by the wind. This is as much as you can do to slow down.

Now helmsman and crew must watch the depth and raise the centreboard as necessary. The rudder stays down for the moment; as the water becomes shallower,

it is raised. The boat meanwhile, depending on wind strength and wave height, is moving in amongst the surf. Helmsman and crew sit on opposite sides to balance the boat. Once the water is less than waist high, one of the crew can get out, followed by the other. Holding on to the boat from outside, they guide it carefully up on to the sand, before pulling it right out on to the beach. Choose a place which is as free of large stones as possible, to avoid damaging the hull.

Everything is prepared with the boat pointing head-to-wind

The crew turns the boat so it is pointing in the right direction to sail away from the beach

Launching from a beach against the wind

A dinghy is often launched from a jetty, but in some areas it is necessary to launch from a beach. On a beach an onshore wind can be accompanied by waves and surf. Launching then has its dangers. A helmsman and crew who are not used to working together would do better to wait for better conditions for their first beach launch.

The sails are hoisted on the beach beforehand, with the boat facing head-to-wind. The sheets are freed right off, so that the boat cannot be blown over. Then the boat is pulled across the sand into the water. The crew holds on to the side and the helmsman at the stern. In this fashion they can hold the boat head-to-wind even in waves. The centreboard and rudder

The crew climbs on board, followed by the helmsman who pushes the boat forward as he does so

Centreboard and rudder blade are lowered as soon as the water is deep enough

The boat sails away on the tack that will take it farthest from the beach

blade are still raised. When the boat is afloat the crew jumps into the boat. The helmsman pushes off firmly before climbing in, preferably over the stern.

Everything has to be done smoothly at this point. The centreboard is put down as far as the depth of water will allow; the sails are sheeted in; and the rudder blade is lowered as and when possible. The

boat needs to be kept moving now, to prevent the waves from driving it back towards the beach. This means that if you are beating to windward you should not sail too close to the wind, but choose whichever tack enables you to sail slightly more of a reaching course. The boat can then pick up speed to carry it through the waves.

45

A line of boats is towed out to the start of a race. The boats are tied one behind the other. In this situation, the tow ropes should be attached to each other

Towing

It frequently happens that dinghies have to be towed out, either singly or together, to the start of a race because of distance or light winds. Several things have to be borne in mind when towing.

Beware! If a planing dinghy is towed at speed, the towing warp must be long so that it does not plough under. The centreboard should be raised

Firstly, when towing a number of boats in a line, it is necessary to ensure that the load on the lines of individual boats does not become too great. If all the dinghies are attached one behind the other, the first boat may sustain damage. This makes it wise to spread the load. To do this, the towing boat can stream a long warp to which the dinghies make

fast individually with a *rolling hitch*. Alternatively, the line from the boat in front can be tied round the mast, and the line of the boat behind made fast to the loop. This to a great extent relieves the strain imposed on the boat by those behind.

When determining the length of the towing warp it is important to make sure that the boat being towed rides comfortably and does not plough into the wave in front. Boats being towed in a line must pay constant attention to steering, so that they do not collide with each other.

Below: several boats attached to a long warp from the towing vessel

Right: the red tow rope is led back to the mast. This is often the safest place to attach it

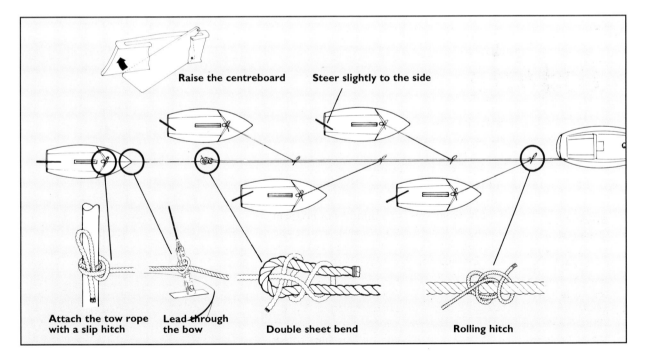

Raise the centreboard   **Steer slightly to the side**

Attach the tow rope with a slip hitch   **Lead through the bow**   **Double sheet bend**   **Rolling hitch**

47

A guide to the boat

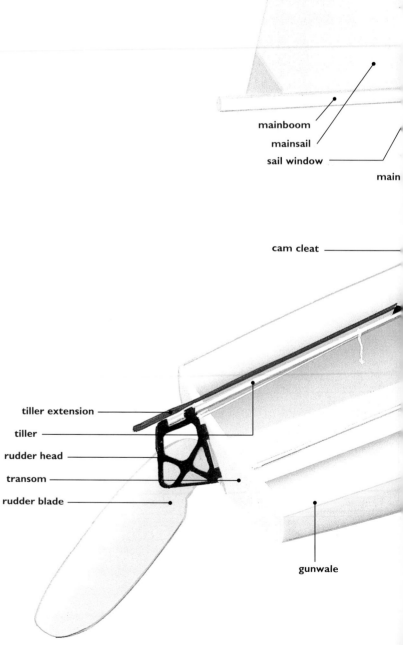

sail batten

mainboom

mainsail

sail window

main

cam cleat

tiller extension

tiller

rudder head

transom

rudder blade

gunwale

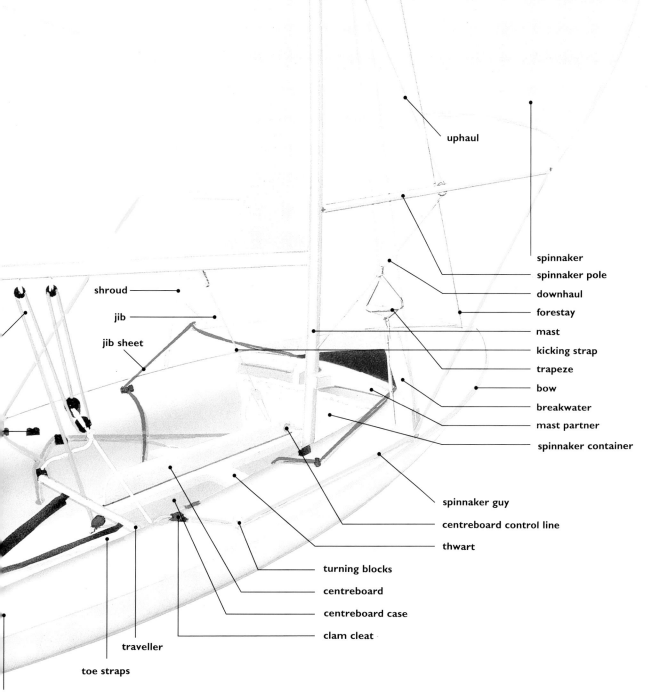

uphaul

spinnaker

spinnaker pole

downhaul

forestay

mast

kicking strap

trapeze

bow

breakwater

mast partner

spinnaker container

shroud

jib

jib sheet

spinnaker guy

centreboard control line

thwart

turning blocks

centreboard

centreboard case

clam cleat

traveller

toe straps

ancy tank

Centreboard system. A metal centreplate is usually raised and lowered by means of lines led to either side of the cockpit

Centreboards

If the wind is coming from astern the boat is pushed along by it, but if the wind is coming from the side it pushes the boat sideways. To reduce this effect, a boat needs a suitable surface underwater to lessen this sideways drift. Leeway cannot be eliminated entirely, but can be kept within limits by the shape and size of the surface presented.

The device used by dinghies to reduce leeway is the centreboard (or metal centreplate), which can be set in various positions. For running before the wind it is raised almost fully; for sailing close-hauled it is lowered. There is a great variety of actual centreboard arrangements. The two main categories are swinging centreboards, in which the board pivots around a bolt near the forward end of the centreboard case, and daggerboards, which are inserted into the case from above. The advantage of the swinging centreboard is that it can be smoothly adjusted while sailing, often by means of a line. Daggerboards are normally used on smaller dinghies.

Inserting a daggerboard into its case

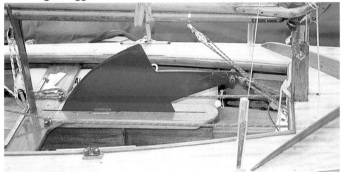

Curved metal centreplate

1 Centreboard raised nearly fully, for running before the wind

2 Centreboard half-down, for reaching

3 Centreboard right down, for sailing close-hauled or beating

4 In this position the centreboard offers the most resistance to leeway

Rudders

An assortment of lifting rudders and a transom-mounted fixed rudder

Lining up the rudder over its mountings on the transom

The rudder is dropped into place on its mountings

In contrast to cars, which follow in the direction set by the front wheels when the steering is applied, a boat is steered by making its stern swing to one side. Otherwise the principle is much the same. Putting the tiller across causes the rudder to turn about its vertical axis. The difference in pressure between the two sides of the blade pushes the stern sideways.

For dinghies, which are often launched from the beach or from a trailer, the established (more practical) type is the lifting rudder. It can be raised or lowered, pivoting around a bolt in the rudder head. The advantage of this is that the helmsman does not have to wait until the water is deep enough to attach the entire assembly of rudder and tiller, but can put the blade down progressively as the water becomes deeper. Lifting rudders can be adjusted during sailing using a line which can be cleated to hold the blade in any position.

Larger boats do not have lifting rudders. Their fixed rudders are either mounted on the transom or fitted beneath the hull on a shaft which passes down through the hull.

Rudder arrangement on a larger boat

If the water is shallow the blade is left in the raised position

If the water is deep enough the blade is lowered with the aid of the control line

The line is secured by a cleat on the tiller to keep the blade down

Mainsheet systems

The mainsheet operates through a system of pulleys (blocks), which are necessary to control a large sail like the mainsail. The larger the mainsail, the greater the force that the mainsheet system will have to supply, and so the more blocks it will need to have. (A winch is essential on larger yachts, because the forces are simply too great to manage by hand.)

The mainsheet is used to control the horizontal angle of the mainsail to the wind. But since the vertical angle of the main-

sheet varies as it is pulled in and let out, the vertical tension on the sail will also vary. Many boats therefore have a *traveller*, which also allows a limited degree of alteration of sail angle without adjusting the sheet. The traveller carries the lower block of the mainsheet and runs on a track, so it can slide the full width of the cockpit without altering the vertical angle of the sheet. So by maintaining the downward pull on the sheet the mainsail is kept under the same tension.

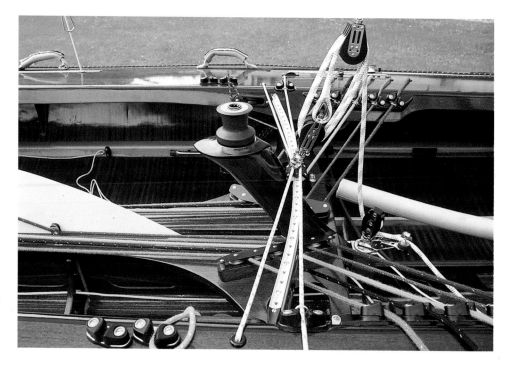

View of the cockpit of an older boat. The curved track runs across the full width. The traveller carrying the lower block of the mainsheet slides across it

Travellers are found less often on smaller boats and dinghies, because the same effect can be achieved in different ways. Some dinghies have a vertical triangle of wire rigged across the boat. The lower block of the mainsheet is attached to the top of the triangle. Mainsail tension is regulated by means of the *kicking-strap* (see page 56). As the sail is brought in and let out it retains its tension because the boom is prevented from lifting by the kicking-strap. This means that the complex system of lines and the whole traveller assembly can be dispensed with, which helps to keep weight down.

Left: the mainsheet system on this 420 dinghy consists of two converging wire strops. The lower block of the mainsheet is attached to the apex

Left: mainsheet track, traveller, control lines and mainsheet block

Above: a swivel block for the bottom end of the mainsheet. The cam cleat makes it easy to secure the sheet and release it quickly

55

Kicking-straps

An efficient kicking-strap arrangement, a combination of a lever and pulley

If the mainsail is sheeted right in, or nearly so, the pull on the mainsheet is enough to hold the boom down. But when the mainsail is let out as the boat bears away, the sheet loses its vertical restraining effect because the pull on the sheet is more horizontal. The sail could then twist out of shape towards the top. Kicking-straps are employed to prevent this. They continue to hold the boom down as the sail is let out.

Since the kicking-strap is fitted near the forward end of the boom and exerts its pull diagonally, its leverage is not great. This means that the principle of mechanical advantage has to be applied to achieve enough tension and an effective lever or pulley system must be used. A whole variety of systems are used to create effective kicking-straps, but they all have the same function of preventing the boom from lifting.

It is easier on large yachts, as the distance between the boom and the deck is greater, and the angle of the kicking-strap can be more vertical.

The effect of the kicking-strap in maintaining the shape of the sail. In the left-hand picture the mainsheet is eased further out. Despite this the boom is not lifting

Below: a simple kicking-strap on an Optimist dinghy

Above left: a three-part pulley serves as a kicking-strap on this traditional wooden dinghy

Left: a sophisticated system consisting of a perforated lever, plus two sets of control lines, for coarse adjustment and fine tuning

57

Self-bailer in
operation with
the boat in
motion. The
closed bailer
causes almost no
drag

Self-bailers

Self-bailers are devices which remove water by suction from a moving boat. They are hinged metal chutes attached to the underside of the boat, which close flush with the hull. If water gets into the boat the self-bailers can be pushed down. The bailer then forms a wedge-shaped recess in the bottom of the boat. The movement of the boat through the water causes suction which draws water out through the opening at the back. Most bailers have a flap over the opening which is closed by water pressure from outside, so that water cannot enter when the boat slows down.

In the stern of lightweight dinghies there are also often *transom flaps*, which are much more effective at removing large amounts of water after a capsize. These flaps are usually held closed with shock-cord when not required. On dinghies with a double-bottom so the floor of the cockpit is above water level, the transom can even be left completely open because water will not enter.

Self-bailers enable a boat to be emptied quickly even after a capsize, so that sailing can be resumed as normal. The photograph above shows how self-bailers operate. When closed, they cause no friction; when open, water is sucked rapidly out of the boat as it sails along.

Left: the transom drains are opened to let out water on land

Below: transom flaps will remove a lot of water in an emergency

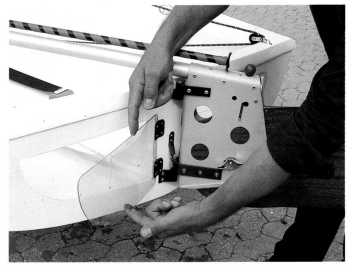

Left: bailer seen from inside. The handle is to open and close it

Above left: bailer seen from outside. When open it projects beneath the hull

Above: perspex transom flaps held shut by shock-cord

Hiking aids

Trapezing is one of the most exhilarating experiences that sailing has to offer. It is also less tiring than sitting out

The boat will sail better if it is kept upright. So the force of the wind should be counterbalanced by crew weight on the windward side. The greater the angle of heel, the more helmsman and crew must lean (hike) out.

At full stretch on the trapeze. To keep your balance bend the back leg and keep the front one straight

Below: putting your feet under the toe straps supports the body while sitting out

In addition, fast planing dinghies may also have a *trapeze*. This consists of two wires, one on either side of the boat, running from high up on the mast down to deck level. The crew wears a *trapeze harness* which can be hooked on to the end of the wire. He or she can then put their feet on the outside edge of the sidedeck, where it meets the hull, and stretch out over the water using their whole weight to maximum effect. The length of the trapeze wires should be adjusted so that the body is at right-angles to the mast when fully outstretched. This maximizes the righting moment.

But it is quite enough for the beginner to use the toe straps. They should be adjusted so that it is possible to sit out with legs slightly bent and the back of the thigh against the outer edge of the sidedeck.

The hook on the harness goes through the ring on the trapeze. This one includes an adjustment for length. The shock-cord holds the trapeze when not in use

61

Wind indicators

The wind indicators of boats meeting on different courses will not point in the same direction. The true wind is the same, but the apparent wind is different

If the sails are to be correctly trimmed to match the wind at any given moment you must be aware of the exact wind direction. An aid to achieving this is a wind indicator. Usually this is a small flag, sometimes called a *burgee*, flown at the masthead. When running before the wind, it points forwards; sailing close-hauled, it points almost straight behind. It is sometimes necessary to find a way of keeping it clear of obstructions, like lights or masthead fittings, which would interfere with its efficient functioning.

When boats are stationary their burgees indicate the true wind direction. As soon as the boat is under way, however, the boat's motion and the wind combine to create the *apparent* wind. Since the burgee moves with the boat, the wind it indicates is always the apparent one. When running before the wind, the true

Far left: arrow-shaped wind indicator. It is accurate, but easily broken

Left: on gaff-rigged boats, the burgee must be mounted in front of the mast to avoid the gaff

Far left: wind sock. Sometimes used in place of a burgee

Left: a square flag. Formerly it was compulsory to have a square flag in place of a burgee when racing and these are still sometimes seen

and apparent winds are from the same direction, although the apparent wind is weaker than the true wind. Close-hauled, on the other hand, the apparent wind is stronger and meets the boat at a more acute angle than the true wind.

Larger yachts may have anemometers and arrow-shaped wind indicators.

Sail battens

The rear edge (the *leech*) of the mainsail does not follow a direct line from the top of the mast to the end of the boom, but curves outside it. This extra area (the *roach*) would sag if it were not supported by battens. These are made of a variety of materials, usually synthetic, and of varying stiffness. A whole range of widths and degrees of stiffness exists, including tapered battens of laminated construction, with varying flexibility along their length.

On some dinghies the top batten extends right across the sail. This batten can then be used to control the shape of the sail. If compression is applied to the batten when it is inserted, the sail will adopt a more curved shape than if it is simply fitted loose in its pocket. This tension gives the sail the fuller profile useful in light winds. In strong winds a flatter sail shape is desirable, so tension is not applied. The batten pocket may be closed with a Velcro strip, pulled tight to maintain the desired curvature.

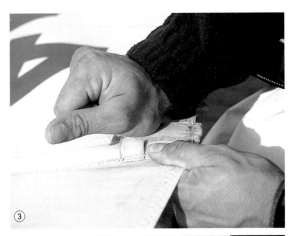

① **The batten is inserted into the pocket**

② **Attached to the sail is a tongue with a Velcro strip**

③ **The tongue is used to tension the sail**

④ **Finally the tongue is slipped through a band**

⑤ **This keeps the batten under compression**

⑥ **Alterations to the tension can still be made**

Rigging
the boat

Rigging fittings

A number of different fittings may be found at the junction of the shrouds or stays and the mast, and again at the attachment between the rigging and the hull. Not only must these fittings be strong enough to withstand the massive loads sometimes imposed on them, but, equally important, they must not weaken the mast at that point. It is essential to spread the load at the junction with the mast. This may be done by attaching the ends of the rigging to projecting fittings on the mast, called tangs, or by inserting a T-shaped terminal into a stainless steel keyhole plate. Another, less common, method is to pass a bolt through the mast and through loops in the ends of the shrouds.

The junction between the rigging and the hull is different. Here there is usually a *chain plate* with a hole in it projecting above the deck. The rigging screws or adjustable rigging links are attached to this with a clevis pin, secured by a split pin. The end of the shrouds or stays has either a swaged terminal or a loop formed around a *thimble*. The latter is held together by a ferrule clamped tight with special pliers.

All movable parts must be prevented from working loose by inserting split pins or binding with copper wire.

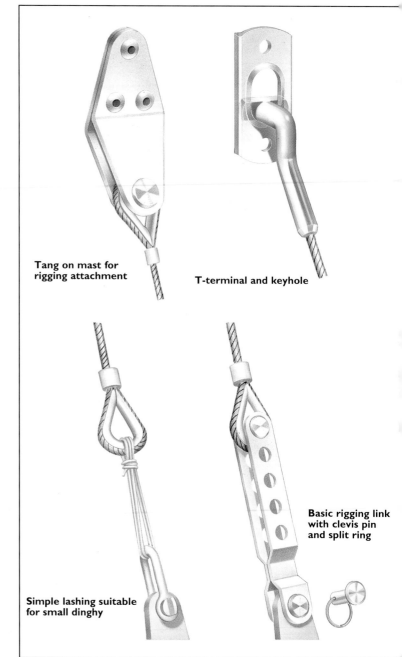

Tang on mast for rigging attachment

T-terminal and keyhole

Simple lashing suitable for small dinghy

Basic rigging link with clevis pin and split ring

68

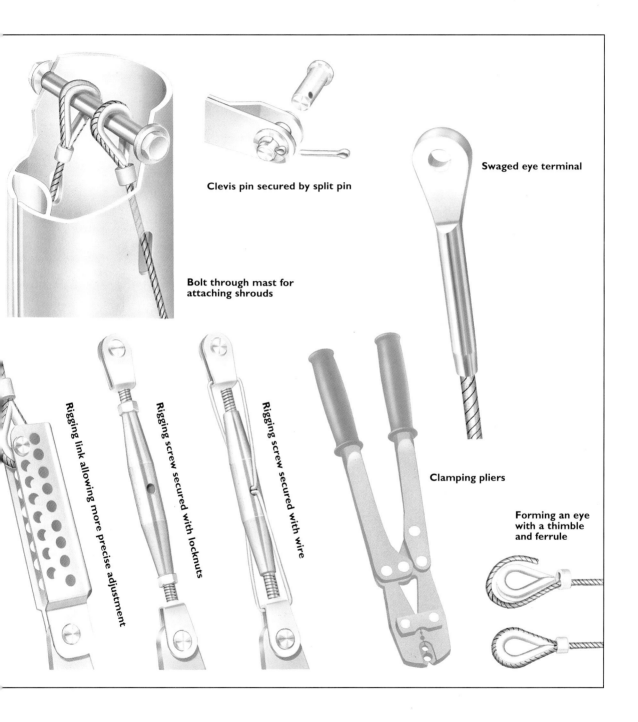

Bolt through mast for
attaching shrouds

Clevis pin secured by split pin

Swaged eye terminal

Rigging link allowing more precise adjustment

Rigging screw secured with locknuts

Rigging screw secured with wire

Clamping pliers

Forming an eye
with a thimble
and ferrule

Tuning the rig

The bend in the mast of these racing keelboats can be altered at the touch of a control line

Most boats today, in contrast to the old days, have what is termed a flexible rig. This does not mean that the mast flexes easily or randomly, but rather that it can be adjusted and then fixed in the desired position.

Two controls for adjusting the mast are the *spreaders*, which can be angled aft to a greater or lesser degree according to the amount of mast bend required, and wedges, which can be inserted into the *mast gate*, between the forward edge of the mast and the foredeck. The more the spreaders are angled back and the fewer wedges are inserted between mast and deck, the more the mast can bend.

Mast bend like this makes the mainsail flatter which is desirable for sailing close-hauled in strong winds. Tightening the kicking-strap also helps, as well as reducing the twist in the sail. The *Cunningham hole* adjustment which tightens the leading edge of the mainsail also helps to open the leach and reduce the heeling moment of the boat in medium to strong winds.

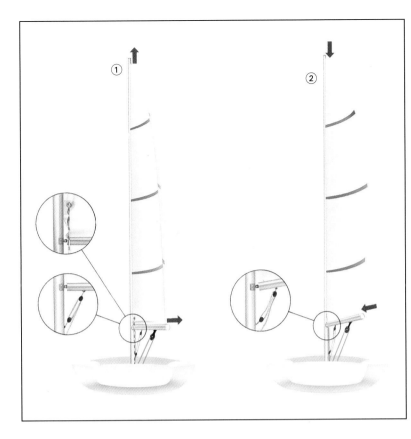

① **Mainsail flattened using the Cunningham hole and kicking-strap**

② **Without a tight kicking-strap the sail twists off towards the top**

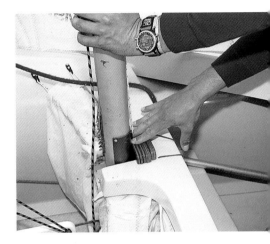

Below: the effect of spreader angle and mast wedges (shown above) on mast bend

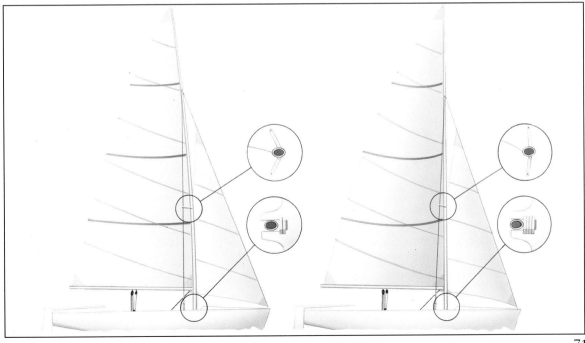

Stepping the mast

The rigging may be kept lashed to the mast during stepping

Stepping (erecting) the mast in a dinghy does not usually present any difficulty, because it is very light. Only in windy conditions is extra care needed because the mast will sway about once it is upright. The whole mast, together with its shrouds and stays, is lifted and the *heel* (base of the mast) is placed in the *mast step* on the floor of the cockpit. Then the mast is pushed into place in the mast gate which holds it steady temporarily while the shrouds and forestay are fixed to the boat. Finally the mast wedges are inserted at the front of the mast, according to the degree of mast bend required. As we have seen, the more wedges there are between the foredeck and the mast, the less the mast bends.

Lowering the mast on to the mast step

Far left: the mast step has a series of holes for adjusting the mast position

Left: The mast is located in the mast step

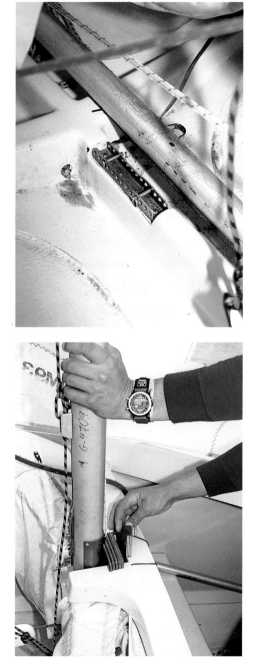

Far left: inserting the mast wedges

Left: attaching the rigging to the hull

Fitting the mainsail

① Feeding the clew into the groove in the boom

② The clew is pulled along the boom to the black band

③ Securing the clew to the end of the boom

④ The tack has been secured at the other end of the boom

⑤ The battens are put in their pockets

⑥ The gooseneck fits into the end of the boom

⑦ The battens are tensioned to suit the wind strength

⑧ Attaching the halyard to the head of the sail

⑨ The mainsail is ready to hoist

Before the sails can be hoisted everything has to be prepared with the boat on land or on the jetty. First you should find the rear lower corner of the sail, the *clew*. Run your hand along the *foot* (lower edge) of the sail to make sure that it is not twisted. Then the foot of the sail is threaded, clew first, into the groove in the boom at the end nearest to the mast and pulled along the length of the boom. Finally the forward lower corner of the sail, the *tack*, is attached at the front end of the boom.

The foot is pulled taut and the clew fastened in position at the back end of the boom. Next you should run your hand along the *luff* (leading edge) of the sail as far as the *head* (top corner) of the sail and push it into the groove in the mast. The main halyard can also be shackled on to the head at this point.

Finally the battens are inserted into their pockets and fastened in position. They serve to stiffen the *leech* (trailing edge) of the sail. The mainsail is then ready to hoist. The only other thing to ensure is that the mainsheet is slackened right off, so that the sail does not catch the wind when hoisted and blow the boat over.

①

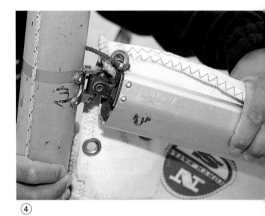

④

⑦

②

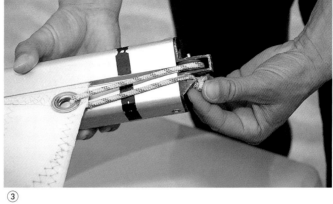

③

⑤

⑥

⑧

⑨

Fitting the jib

A jib has the same basic features as the mainsail, although it is not attached to mast or boom. The first step in fitting it is generally to attach the tack of the jib to the deck immediately behind the forestay. Then work back along the foot of the sail to the clew.

The jibsheet has two parts, one for the port and one for the starboard side. If it is not yet tied on to the clew, now is the time to do so. Often there is a shackle for attaching the jibsheet, instead, although this can whip about when tacking and cause injury. The jibsheets are led back on each side of the mast and passed through the jib *fairleads*. A figure-of-eight knot is tied in the end of the sheets to prevent them slipping out again. Finally the head of the jib has to be attached to the

① **The rolled-up jib is ready on the foredeck. The sheets have been attached**

② **The tack is shackled to the forestay fitting**

③ **The jibsheets are led back either side of the mast**

①

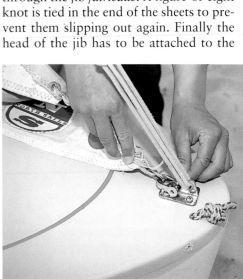

②

③

jib halyard. Before doing this, first glance up and check that the wire is not twisted around the mast or forestay.

Now the jib is ready to hoist. Take care that it is not blown on to the ground or into the water as soon as you let go of it. Some jibs are attached to the forestay by a series of clips along the luff, called *hanks*, which prevents this from happening. Otherwise it should be hoisted as soon as possible.

④ Once through the fairlead, a figure-of-eight knot is tied in the sheet as a stopper

⑤ The sheets are coiled to prevent tangles

⑥ Glance upwards to check that the halyard is not twisted

⑦ The halyard is shackled to the head of the jib

77

Hoisting the sails

① **The jib is hoisted before launching**

② **The crew pulls the mast forward with the forestay so that the jib halyard can be pulled tight**

③ **The dinghy now goes down the slipway into the water**

④ **One person gets on board while the other holds on to the boat from the jetty**

⑤ **The head of the mainsail is inserted into the groove in the mast**

⑥ **Finally the mainsail is hoisted by hauling on the main halyard**

There are different procedures for hoisting sails, depending on whether the boat is already afloat, like a keelboat, or whether it has to be launched like a dinghy. The usual method for dinghies is to hoist the jib first, while the boat is still on land. The advantage of this is that one person can apply weight to the forestay. This enables the proper tension to be put into the jib luff. The jib halyard emerges at the rear of the mast heel. On this boat it has an eye half-way down which simply has to be slipped over a hook to make the halyard secure. Assuming the jibsheets have already been put through the fairleads, the boat can now be launched down the slipway.

7 The loop of the halyard is hooked over the toothed rack

8 The rack allows for different amounts of tension to be put on the halyard

9 The boom is attached to the mast by the gooseneck which allows it to swing in any direction

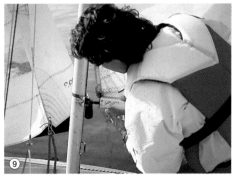

If the area is too crowded for you to sail out easily under the jib alone, a place should be found to hoist the mainsail where the boat can be pointed into the wind. The mainsheet is freed off and the mainsail can then be hoisted.

Sailing with a spinnaker

Hoisting the spinnaker

① **The helmsman stands up with the tiller between his knees**

② **He takes hold of the spinnaker halyard**

③ **The crew throws the spinnaker forward as it is hoisted**

④ **The spinnaker is up. The halyard is secured**

⑤ **The helmsman controls the spinnaker sheets**

Many dinghies have two containers for the spinnaker, one on either side of the mast. If you know in advance which side you will want to hoist it on you can arrange for it to be in the right container.

It is generally easier to hoist the spinnaker on the leeward side of the boat, especially on a reach, because it is sheltered by the mainsail during hoisting. Here, however, for clarity it is being hoisted on the windward side and, as it is a reach, the crew has to throw it forwards to get it round the forestay while the helmsman is hoisting it. Hoisting has to be quick if you do not want the sail to catch the wind before it is right up.

When the spinnaker is up, the pole is fitted to hold it out to windward. The sheet (on the leeward side) and the *guy* (on the windward side) are trimmed to get the sail drawing properly.

⑥ **The crew fits the spinnaker pole to the mast**

⑦ **She takes over control of the guy first then the sheet**

① **On a beam reach, the pole is forward and angled slightly upwards so the sail is flatter in the middle**

② **On a broad reach, the pole is horizontal and pulled back until the luff is about to curl**

③ **On a run, the pole is at right-angles to the boat and the spinnaker is brought as far round to windward as possible**

Trimming the spinnaker

The spinnaker, as you would expect of a large parachute-shaped sail, develops a lot of power when the wind is behind if the pole is rigged at right-angles to the wind and the sail itself is kept as much out of the lee of the mainsail as possible. However, this is still not the quickest way to sail downwind except in very strong winds. It is better, especially if the wind is light, to 'tack' downwind keeping the boat on a broad-reaching course. The spinnaker pole is then angled farther forward. The correct position is found by

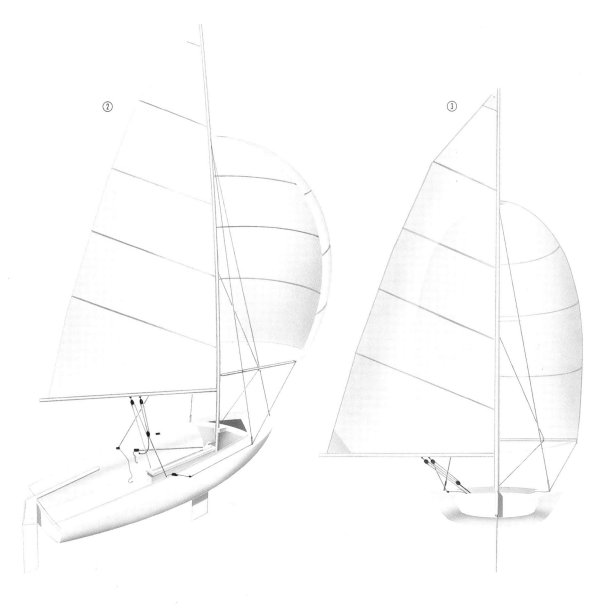

experiment, pulling the pole back until the luff of the spinnaker is almost ready to collapse. The foot of the sail will be passing somewhere near the forestay.

On a beam reach, or even a close reach if the spinnaker can still be managed, the pole is eased forward as far as the forestay and angled slightly upwards.

This has the effect of pulling the sail very flat across its middle section which, with the apparent wind coming from ahead, improves the airflow around the spinnaker and makes it more efficient. But the pole should not actually touch the forestay or it will disturb the luff of the jib and affect the airflow over the rest of the sail.

Gybing the spinnaker

A number of operations have to be co-ordinated when gybing under spinnaker. This manoeuvre can easily lead to a capsize if mistakes are made, especially in windy conditions. First the dinghy is ·brought on to a course with the wind directly behind. While bearing away, the pole is kept at right-angles to the wind by pulling in the guy. When the main boom goes over, the pole is still on its original side.

As soon as the mainsail has gybed, the spinnaker pole is detached from the mast and hooked on to the guy (which until now was the sheet). The pole is now attached to both bottom corners of the spinnaker. It is then detached from the old guy (which is now the sheet) and hooked on to the mast fitting.

I Before the gybe the pole should be angled forward at about 45°

While the crew is occupied at the mast, the helmsman has to control the spinnaker sheets as well as steer the boat. When the gybe is complete the boat can luff up on to a new course.

4 The mainsail swings across the boat

5 The crew first takes the pole off the ma

2 The sheet is eased about the same amount as the guy

3 The helmsman bears away to gybe the mainsail

6 Finally the pole is put back on the mast

7 The helmsman trims the spinnaker until the manoeuvre is complete

Lowering the spinnaker

In light winds lowering the spinnaker presents no problem, but the operation becomes more difficult in stronger winds. Good teamwork is the key to success. It is not enough for the helmsman to concentrate on the mainsheet and steering a course; he must contribute his share to the success of the operation and take over tasks which the crew would normally carry out.

If the heel of the boat allows, he takes the tiller between his knees to give him both hands free for action. The crew takes down the spinnaker pole, while the helmsman releases the spinnaker halyard. At this point everything happens very quickly. The crew grabs hold of the sail, gathers it in and stows it in the windward spinnaker bag.

① **The helmsman holds the tiller between his knees, while the crew releases the spinnaker pole**

④ **The helmsman continues lowering, while the crew bundles the sail into the bag**

② **The helmsman frees the halyard and the crew stows the pole away**

③ **The helmsman starts to lower the spinnaker. The crew catches hold of the tack**

⑤ **When the sail is down the helmsman lets go of the halyard**

⑥ **The crew tidies up, as the helmsman gets the boat sailing normally again**

Further
techniques

Jib fairlead position

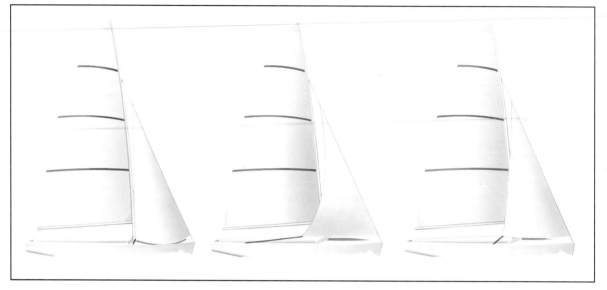

The effect of moving the jib fairlead. Too far forward (left), too far back (centre), correct (right)

The jib fairleads are often mounted on a track so they can be moved backwards or forwards a certain amount, if necessary.

Shifting the fairlead forward or back will alter the angle at which the sheet meets the jib, affecting the set of the sail. If, for example, the fairlead is too far back, the sheeting angle will be nearly parallel to the deck. The foot of the jib is pulled tight; the leech is slack and bows outwards. In the opposite case (fairlead too far forward), the leech is pulled down tight, but the foot of the sail bows out. As a rule of thumb, the fairlead position should distribute tension evenly between leech and foot.

A useful guide to trimming the jib is provided by *telltales* (strands of wool attached to both sides of the sail near the luff). If both the inner and outer telltales along the whole length of the luff stream smoothly across the sail, then the sheeting (including fairlead position) is correct. If the windward telltale flutters, the sheet needs to be pulled in; the leeward telltale indicates the opposite.

The matter is more difficult if the middle of the sail looks correct, but the *leeward* telltale at the top and the *windward* one at the bottom are fluttering. Then it is the twist of the sail which is wrong. The fault is in the fairlead position. When this

92

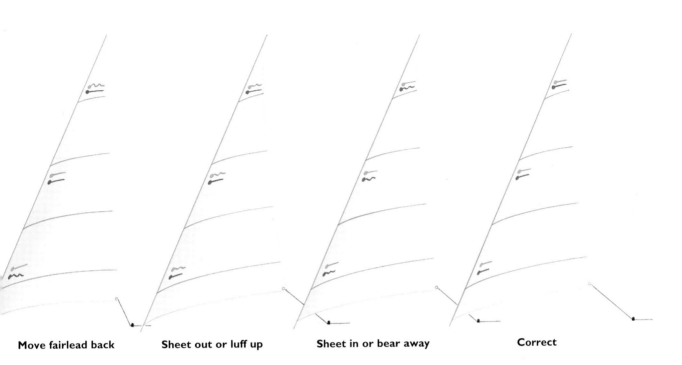

Move fairlead back **Sheet out or luff up** **Sheet in or bear away** **Correct**

happens, the fairlead must be moved along the track until a smooth airflow is achieved down the whole length of the luff, so that both inner and outer telltales stream evenly. In the case we have just described, the sail is in too tight at the top (so the leeward telltale flutters) and not tight enough at the bottom (so the windward telltale flutters). This necessitates moving the fairlead further back along the track to apply greater tension to the foot. This also releases tension on the leech, flattening the lower portion of the sail.

Practice will, in fact, soon demonstrate which is the most effective way of achiev-

ing an efficient set to the jib. When the boat is not sailing close to the wind there is some advantage in being able to move the fairleads further outboard. But extra blocks are required if adjustment of the fairlead position in both dimensions is to be possible.

Whether and in which directions the fairlead can be moved is, in any case, not just a matter of the system available, but also of the specifications laid down for a particular class of boat. The rules of some classes of dinghy do not allow the fairleads to be adjusted at all.

What telltales mean. Ideally both leeward (shown in blue) and windward telltales (shown in red) should be streaming smoothly back across the sail

Teamwork

①**The boat heels. The crew goes out on the trapeze**

Above all, sailing a two-person dinghy involves teamwork; success depends on the crew members working well together. It is also true that the helmsman generally has the dominant role. He or she has charge of the tiller and the mainsheet. During spinnaker hoisting or lowering, it is the helmsman who controls the halyard. To do this, he or she holds the tiller between the knees to free both hands for action.

The crew normally controls the jib sheet and maintains the balance of the boat by shifting his or her weight on to the trapeze or the sidedeck as needed. During spinnaker work the crew controls the spinnaker sheet and also prepares the sail, feeds it out, gathers it in and stows it away. The crew should keep a constant lookout for other boats, for wind changes, or for the next buoy when racing, except when controlling the spinnaker; then it is the helm's job.

Before a manoeuvre, the helmsman must give the appropriate warning, so that the crew is prepared.

④**Both crew are on the windward side**

94

② **The crew alone cannot keep the boat upright**   ③ **The helmsman starts to come across the boat**

⑤ **A sudden lull. The crew comes in from the trapeze**   ⑥ **Another gust. Both helm and crew are at full stretch**

Surfing in a following sea

When dinghies plane they can sometimes travel faster than the waves. But first the stern has to be lifted by the crest of a following sea. The principle then is similar to that of riding a surfboard.

When the wave approaches from behind, bear away down it and shift your weight slightly towards the front of the boat as you do so, to try and keep it on the face of the wave. As the boat surfs off down the front of the wave it accelerates dramatically and the apparent wind comes

more from ahead. So it is essential to pull the sheets in as you gain speed. Otherwise the sails will start to flap and you will slow down again. If you find yourself overtaking the wave ahead you should luff slightly, sheeting the sails in even more, because if you start to climb the back of the wave you will also lose speed.

Surfing is exhilarating, but it requires constant attention to weight distribution, the sheets and steering, luffing up and bearing away as necessary. Of course,

you may not be sailing in exactly the direction you wanted to go, but waiting for the next wave to come up behind gives you an opportunity to compensate by luffing up somewhat.

To take full advantage of a following sea the helmsman weaves from a reach to a run, and back again. In essence, when you are going down the face of a wave, bear away; when you find yourself in the trough or climbing up the back of a wave, luff up

Capsizing

A capsize is not always preventable. It may be caused by an exceptionally hard gust which simply overpowers the dinghy and capsizes it. In days gone by, that meant the end of the day's sailing. But the modern materials and construction of most dinghies give them enough buoyancy to be righted fairly easily.

Once a dinghy is upright again, the water remaining in the cockpit is sucked out as it gets under way again. So a properly equipped sailor, wearing a lifejacket or buoyancy aid, need not fear a capsize as long as the weather is pleasant.

One of the commonest causes of a capsize is an accidental gybe, when the boom swings across the boat suddenly and unexpectedly. The weight of the helmsman on the lee side combines with the

④ If the boat can be prevented from going over any further than this, righting will be easier

③ The boat goes over. With more luck, the crew might have got up on to the side of the boat without getting wet

force of the wind on the sail to upset the boat. It capsizes and at first rests with the mast parallel to the water. With sufficiently quick reflexes, it is possible to right a capsize at this point without even getting wet.

The helmsman or crew need to prevent the mast from going under water. So one member swims round to the bow, supporting the forestay while the other takes up a position standing on the centre-board. The whole process is easier if the boat is turned into the wind. Once the dinghy has started to come upright, it reaches a point when it suddenly rights itself. At this point what matters is to prevent it from going past the vertical and capsizing again in the opposite direction.

On no account should anyone leave a capsized boat. It is fatally easy to underestimate the difficulty of swimming ashore.

② **The helmsman goes overboard and there is nothing the crew can do as the mainsail starts to gybe across**

① **The boat heels to windward with the wind behind. This tends to make it bear away and heel even further**

Righting a capsize

Climbing promptly over the side and on to the centreboard on capsizing is the way to avoid even getting wet. It also helps stop the mast from sinking under water, so that the boat cannot turn right over. The other member of the crew, meanwhile, swims to the bow to support the forestay and helps prevent the mast from going under water. Once the mast is clear of the water, the best policy is to wait for the boat to turn round with its bow into the wind, so that the wind exerts no force on the sails as the boat is righted.

It is important to free off all the sheets as far as they will go, as well as the kicking strap, so that the boat is less likely to get blown over again. When the dinghy springs upright it must be prevented from promptly capsizing again, so both members of the crew must use their weight to balance it. The safest place to climb back into the boat is over the side near the shroud. With one person in the boat to stop it from bearing away and sailing off, the other could climb in over the stern.

① **The heaviest crew member climbs over the side on to the centreboard**

② **He uses his weight to lever the boat upright**

③ **As the boat starts to right itself he climbs back into the cockpit**

④ **As the boat springs upright he is able to stop it going over the other way**

⑤ **He helps the crew to climb in over the stern**

⑥ **Meanwhile, the sheets and kicking strap are freed right off to prevent further capsizes**

①

④

③

⑤ ⑥

①　②

Righting an upside-down boat

A boat that has turned completely upside-down is a much tougher proposition. The weight of one person alone will not be enough to right the boat. So one crew member holds on to the centreboard, with his feet on the underside of the edge of the sidedeck. To provide more leverage, the other crew member holds on to him, as the dinghy slowly turns back upright. Both crew remain in this position until the mast is parallel to the water. Then the bow can be turned into the wind, so it does not catch the sails as the boat comes upright.

The main part of the task has now been accomplished. The helmsman keeps hanging on to the centreboard. The crew goes to the bow. The remaining steps are as for a normal capsize.

⑤

④

⑥

① The boat has turned right over

② The helmsman climbs on to the hull and takes hold of the centreboard

③ The crew holds on to the helmsman

④ The boat starts to turn back upright again

⑤ When the mast is nearly parallel to the water, the crew moves to the bow

⑥ The rest of the operation is as for a normal capsize

Trapeze technique

To keep a light dinghy sailing at its best in all conditions the crew, who are the movable human 'ballast', must react continually to fluctuations in the force of the wind. If the wind shows marked variation in direction as well as strength, the helmsman must also maintain the angle of the sails to it by turning the boat to match the wind. So constant attention to course, as well as balance, is required. If there are waves, the helmsman must also make sure that the boat meets them in the best way, taking them gently without abrupt loss of speed. 'Feel' is needed to sail a boat well in conditions like this, and that develops with practice.

As soon as the crew notices the wind slackening and the trapeze getting closer to the water, she must bend her knees to reduce the 'righting moment' of her weight on the wire. The helmsman will often be able to help by bearing away a little, to increase the apparent wind strength. If this cannot be done because the boat cannot head any higher into the wind, the only alternative is to reduce the amount of weight on the windward side.

The interaction of crew and helmsman must be honed to perfection if they want to measure up to the best in the fleet. The crew must develop as keen a feeling for the trim of the boat as the helmsman and must keep mobile so that the dinghy makes best use of the available wind and is slowed down as little as possible by the waves.

The best way of practising this is for the crew to hike out fully and the helmsman to try to influence the trim of the boat by changes of course alone. Or for the helmsman to keep to one course while the crew tries to maintain the trim of the boat solely by the use of his or her weight.

③ **The crew bends her legs to reduce the righting moment**

104

① **Sailing fast and upright with the crew out on the trapeze**

② **A slight windshift and the helmsman bears away a little**

④ **The helmsman luffs slightly to meet a wave**

⑤ **A sudden lull. The boat slows down and the crew must come back into the boat**

① The trapeze is hooked on while sitting on the sidedeck

② Bend the leg nearest the bow

⑤ Both feet are against the edge of the sidedeck

⑥ The forward leg is kept straight while the other is flexed
In waves it would be better to have the feet farther apart

Getting out on the trapeze

③ **The foot is braced against the edge of the sidedeck**　④ **The body moves out as the leg is straightened**

⑦ **The ring is lowered by means of the small block and tackle below the handle**

Trapezing is far less strenuous than most beginners imagine. The first important point is to make sure that the trapeze harness fits and the position of the hook is roughly at your centre of gravity (just below the navel). The shoulder straps should be under tension when you are leaning right back, so as to take the strain off your back.

Getting out is done by putting the forward foot against the edge of the sidedeck and then straightening the leg. The other leg follows. The triangular handle can be used for assistance. The height of the trapeze can be adjusted by using a different part of the ring or a special pulley arrangement as here. A right-angle between your outstretched body and the mast is the ideal.

⑧ **Height adjustment. Here the ring is too high**

Heaving-to

① Sailing close-hauled. The jib is pulled in tight

② The boat tacks. The jibsheet is left cleated

③ The jib is backed. The mainsheet is freed off

Heaving-to is a manoeuvre which enables the boat to lie as nearly stationary in the water as possible. The boat is then said to be *hove-to*.

One way to approach it is by sailing close-hauled. Sheet the jib in tight and cleat it. Then tack. As the boat comes round, the jib will be backed and the boat will slow down to the point where the rudder has little effect. The bow will turn away from the wind. The mainsheet is freed right off, so the mainsail has little effect either. Now the tiller is put over as if you were going to luff. The rudder and the backed jib cancel each other out and the boat drifts slowly to leeward.

The drift of the boat even has a slight calming effect on the waves. Heaving-to is a way of being able to carry out a repair at leisure or relax while waiting for the start of a race.

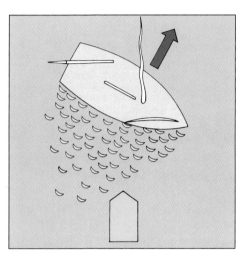

④ **The jib pushes the bow away from the wind**

⑤ **The tiller is pushed to leeward to counteract the jib**

Man overboard

① **Sailing fast on a close reach**

② **A toe strap breaks and the crew goes overboard**

③ **Keeping an eye on the crew, the helmsman bears away immediately**

④ **He sails on to make a bit of room for manoeuvre before tacking**

If someone, or something, falls overboard you will have to sail back to them on a course that permits you to stop the boat immediately to leeward of them. To be successful, you must begin your approach at the right point. The best method is to sail away on a reach, tack round and return to the casualty on a reach. Finally, you stop the boat by shooting up head-to-wind.

⑤ **After tacking he
sails back on a
reach, aiming to
leeward of the crew**

⑥ **At what he judges
is the right moment
he luffs up**

⑦ **The boat is head-
to-wind, still moving
slowly ahead**

⑧ **The boat comes
to a stop just to
leeward of the crew**

Roll-tacking

A boat loses speed as it tacks because it is not sailing while the wind is coming from ahead. In light winds, in particular, the boat may have barely enough momentum to carry it through the turn. This makes roll-tacking a useful technique. Rolling the boat to windward before and after tacking gives the boat a little extra forward motion.

① **Sailing close-hauled in a light wind the boat is deliberately heeled to leeward**

② **The helmsman moves up to windward as he prepares to tack**

③ As he starts to tack the helmsman sits out to windward and the crew moves across to join him

④ The boat rolls to windward

⑤ The helmsman does not move until the boom swings across

⑥ As the sails begin to fill on the new tack, the helmsman moves up to windward

⑦ The helmsman sits out. The boat rolls back to windward again

⑧ When the manoeuvre is finished the boat is back on an even keel

Heavy weather sailing

A 'strong' wind, according to meteorologists, starts at force 6, as defined by the internationally accepted Beaufort Scale. 'Heavy weather' might be said not to start until force 7, but for dinghy sailors that is far beyond anything they can normally deal with. For an inexperienced sailor the limit comes around force 4 to 5.

When there is a danger of strong winds it is even more important to check and recheck all gear carefully, to wear a buoyancy aid, and not to sail off on your own. While sailing, a close eye should be kept on developments in the weather.

The excitement of racing under spinnaker in a strong wind

The sails should be adjusted absolutely flat for beating. The centreboard can be raised a little, to shift the centre of lateral resistance aft. A critical situation can often arise just after tacking, if the boat comes to a standstill. Then, with no way on, it is not yet possible to steer and, with the wind now coming from the side, there is great danger of a capsize.

When the boat begins to plane, the crew on the trapeze should move aft, close to the helmsman, which helps the bow to lift and improves the ride in choppy seas.

When the wind is behind, the crew moves back on the trapeze to help the bow to lift

For windy conditions the mainsail is set as flat as possible

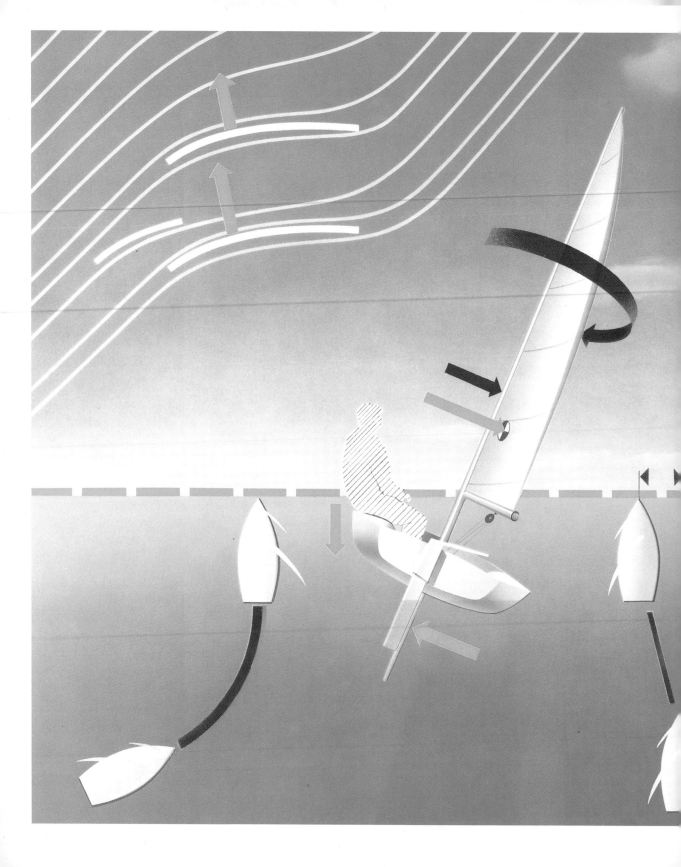

The theory of sailing

Sails as wind resistance

The earliest form of sailing was based on using the wind simply to push the boat along. The sail area was arranged as much at right-angles to the wind as possible, and the greater the available sail area, the greater the resistance offered to the wind, so the more power was available for propulsion. But when the wind is from the side, this method of propulsion ceases to operate and the boat is only pushed sideways. With sails (and underwater hull shapes) like those of early vessels, it was impossible to make progress into the wind.

Even with the wind dead behind, the shape of the sail, or sails, is important. It will soon become obvious to anyone who tries simply setting up a flat surface, like a board, to catch the wind, that this is not the most efficient way of creating wind resistance. The more concave or parachute-like the shape of such a surface, the greater the resistance.

Anyone who wants the wind to push him along should hoist as much canvas as he can and trim the sails to have as much 'belly' as possible. The fullness of the mainsail can be increased by not pulling the foot or the luff tight so that even the otherwise relatively flat sail will become rounded.

With modern sailing dinghies, however, especially if there is not much wind, it can be better not to run directly before the wind, but to steer more of a broad-reaching course with the wind slightly off to one side.

The zigzag course may be longer, but the extra speed can more than make up for it. This is 'tacking downwind'.

It is a mistake to think that a boat is sailing at its fastest with the wind dead behind. The 'head wind' reduces the apparent wind and you notice on board that the wind seems to have dropped. Once the boat is sailing on the wind again it will be quite clear that the wind has not dropped.

The way sails operate in a following wind is more the exception than the rule. Most of the time the wind is from the side, and flows parallel to the curve of the sails. Even spinnakers are so varied in cut today that it is possible to fly one on all points of sailing from a close reach to a run. They, too, can act as aerofoils.

When the wind is dead behind, it meets the sails at right-angles and eddies around behind them. This is different from all other points of sailing

119

Sails as aerofoils

Wind does not just drive boats along ahead of it; the force of the wind can also be used to make progress against it. The first requirement is for surfaces with an aerodynamic shape. In cross-section sails resemble an aircraft wing. When they are trimmed correctly the wind is deflected so delicately from its true direction that an unbroken airflow is maintained. Then 'lift' (to continue the analogy with an aircraft wing) develops on the leeward side of the sail. Lift is a combination of suction on one side and pressure on the other, and acts at right-angles to the sail. There is also another, smaller force acting parallel to the sails caused by friction or the resistance which they offer to the flow of air.

So the force of the wind against the sails consists of two components, lift and resistance. The two could be expressed, by means of a vector diagram, as a single force operating in a direction somewhere between the two. This force would be neither straight ahead nor at right-angles to the boat, but acting diagonally ahead, slightly to leeward.

The boat is being pushed, therefore, not only forwards, but sideways as well. It is possible, by means of yet another vector diagram, to break the diagonal force down again into two more components, representing exactly how much the boat is being pushed forwards and how much at right-angles to its course. If so, it will be found that the size of the sideways force increases as you move from a broad reach to a beam reach to close-hauled.

The sideways force is counteracted to a great extent by the centreboard or, in the case of larger boats, the keel. They do not eliminate it completely, however, and boats still make *leeway*, which means they drift somewhat to leeward even though they appear to be sailing straight ahead.

Far left: on a close reach the airflow is being deflected around the sails, not stopped by them. The result is pressure on the right-hand side of the sails and suction on the left

Above left: lift is the product of the pressure and suction. Resistance is caused by friction. Their combined effect is a diagonal force across to the left-hand corner of the rectangle

Above right: starting with the same diagonal force as before, this vector diagram breaks it down again into two more forces. The forward force drives the boat along; the sideways force causes leeway and heeling

Leeway and heeling

Heeling is the name given to the tendency of the boat to lean sideways under the pressure of the wind and, sometimes, the weight of the crew. Leeway is the sideways drift, or side-slip, as the boat moves forwards through the water. There is no leeway if the wind is behind, but if it comes from over the side or from diagonally ahead leeway and heeling increase.

With the wind behind, the centreboard should be raised, which makes steering easier and the boat go slightly faster

For sailing close-hauled, the centreboard must be lowered because the tendency to leeway is pronounced

Contrary to widespread opinion, a centreboard does not counter heeling. Quite the opposite, it accentuates it. The wind is pushing the boat sideways across the water. The centreboard creates resistance to this below the water, with the result that the boat 'trips over' and heels. Giving way to the wind, on the other hand, by raising the centreboard, reduces heeling, but leeway will carry the boat much further off course. This is the connection between leeway and heeling.

The aim, in practice, is to reduce leeway *and* heeling as much as possible. So when you are close-hauled the centreboard should be right down and the boat kept as upright as possible by the distribution of your weight, and even by easing the sheets in stronger gusts.

Close-hauled, with the centreboard down (bottom), leeway is only slight. With centreboard raised (top), leeway is severe, although heeling is somewhat reduced

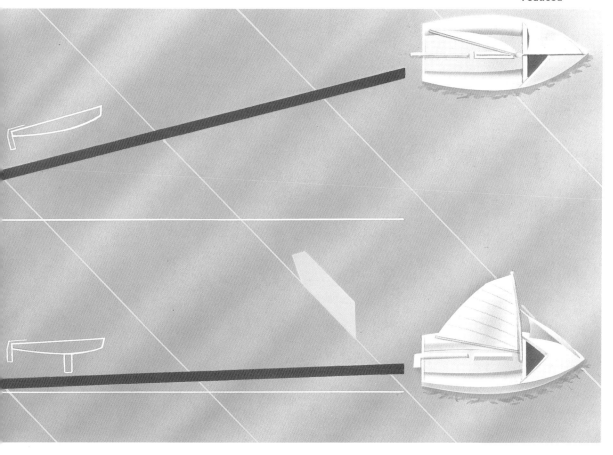

Lee helm and weather helm

Lee and weather helm are opposites. They simply mean that, if the tiller is released when sailing, the boat will turn to lee, or to weather (to windward), of its own accord. Ideally, even if you let go of the tiller, a boat should continue in a straight line. Otherwise you will be having to counter the tendency to change course by use of the rudder the whole time, which will increase drag and slow the boat down.

In theory, a boat will have neutral helm (neither lee helm nor weather helm) if the point where the pressure of the sails is centred, called the *centre of effort* (CE), lies directly above the *centre of lateral resistance* (CLR). Having the CE forward of the CLR will cause lee helm, while weather helm is the result of having the CE further back than the CLR.

Sailing close-hauled this boat carries weather helm as can be seen from the angle of the tiller. In practice, a small amount of weather helm is often desirable

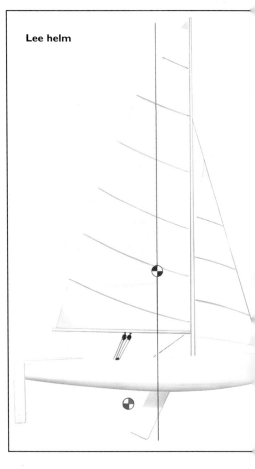

Lee helm

You can change the position of the CLR and the CE in a number of different ways. Sitting further forward in the cockpit, so the bow is deeper in the water than the stern, moves the CLR forward; raising the centreboard slightly, because it swings it towards the stern, moves the CLR back. The CE can be moved forward by stepping the mast, and with it the sails, further forward and by other adjustments, such as reducing the *rake* (backwards slope) of the mast. Very often simpler adjustments, such as easing the mainsheet, are all that is required to reduce excessive weather helm.

In practice, the helmsman will usually find that he has to keep the tiller slightly to windward of the centreline to maintain a straight course. This reflects the fact that most boats have slight weather helm, especially when close-hauled. This is generally because the boat is heeling, so the CE is to leeward of the boat. This tends to make the boat turn to windward, just as a rowing boat would go round in circles if you only rowed it on one side.

In the three examples below (from left to right) the CLR is moved forward by lowering the centreboard and trimming the bow deeper in the water. At the same time the CE is moved back by stepping the mast further back and raking it more towards the stern

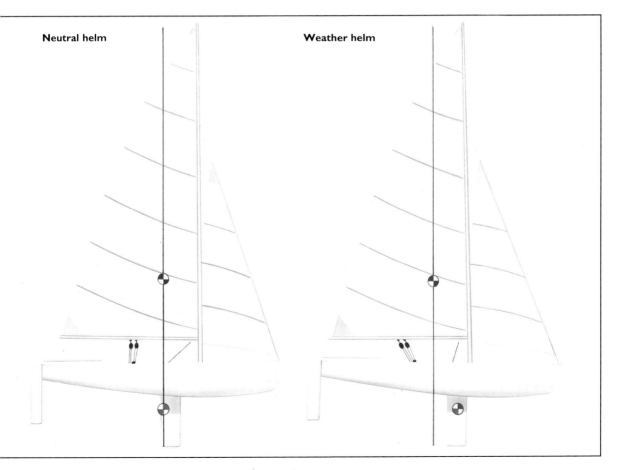

Neutral helm

Weather helm

Planing and displacement hulls

The hull of a boat sinks in the water to a certain point which depends on its weight or *displacement*. When it starts to move, at first the water divides to let it pass and comes together again behind it. A wave develops at the bow and this gets bigger, the faster the boat goes. When it reaches a certain speed the boat simply cannot go any faster without rising up in the water and riding its own bow wave. This is *planing*.

Some boats are too heavy plane and they are known as 'displacement' boats. Other boats, including nearly all modern sailing dinghies, are light enough to plane whenever the wind is strong enough. To promote planing they are designed with comparatively broad, flat bottoms, especially towards the stern. Displacement boats, on the other hand, tend to be more streamlined underwater because they are incapable of skimming across it.

Displacement boats cannot exceed a certain speed (which is related to their length); when a boat is planing it can go, theoretically at least, at any speed. So a planing boat can go faster than a displacement boat of the same length.

126

Before starting to plane the dinghy is sailing as a displacement boat, cutting through the water. Note the bow wave

Below left: when it planes the bow wave disappears beneath the hull and the bow lifts out of the water. The boat skims across the surface

Below: the difference between a hull that is not planing (left) and one that is (right). The blue is the area in contact with the water. The arrows show the direction of water flow

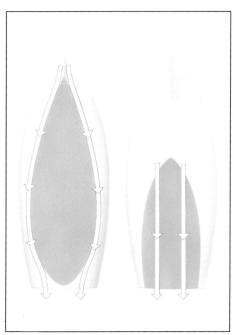

Knots I

Figure-of-eight knot

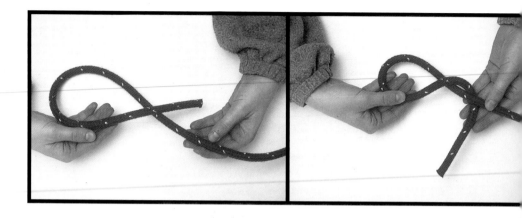

Reef knot

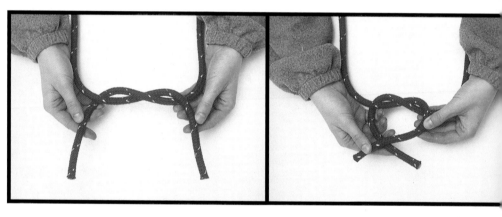

Clove hitch

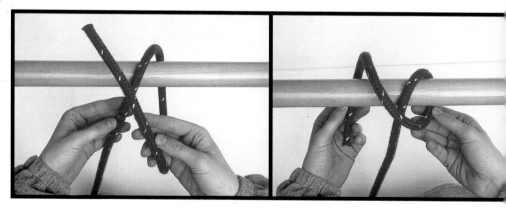

To prevent the end of a sheet from slipping through a fairlead, a figure-of-eight knot is put in the end as a 'stopper knot'. It is easy to undo, which is important for all knots

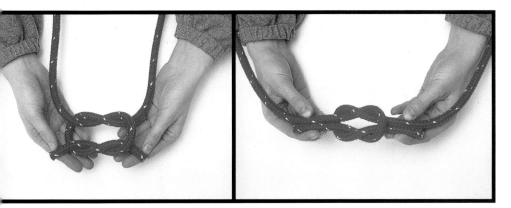

Used to join ropes of equal thickness, it consists of two knots, tied one on top of the other in opposite directions. The finished knot should be neat and symmetrical

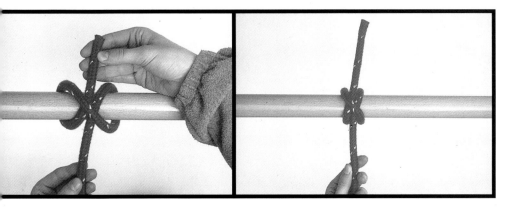

Used to fasten a rope to an object when there will be strain on both sides of the knot. Otherwise it may slip. The rope is passed twice around the object in the same direction, first over itself then underneath.

Knots II

Bowline

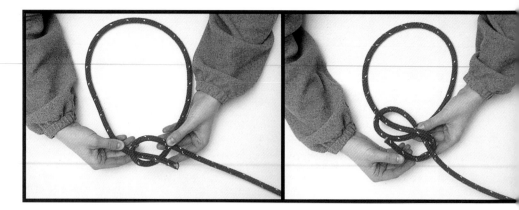

Rolling hitch

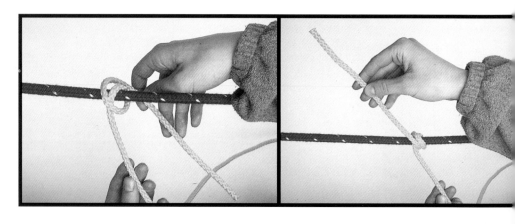

Sheet bend

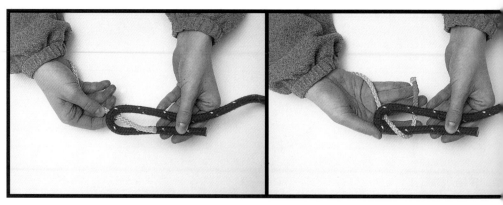

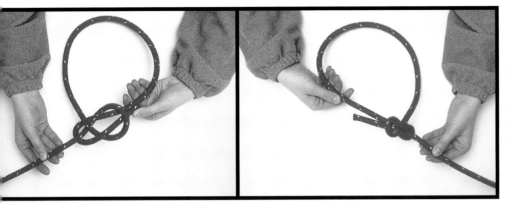

Used to make a loop which will not slip, such as to throw over a post or bollard. The knot can be undone even when it has been subject to a heavy strain

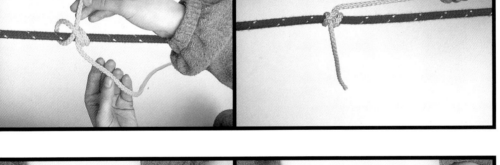

A useful, but not very common knot, used to fasten a rope to the middle of another. The first two turns must be on the side of the knot to which strain will be applied

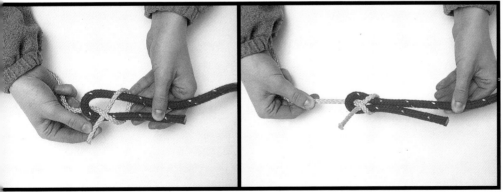

Used instead of a reef knot to join ropes of unequal thickness. A double sheet bend, where the end of the light rope is passed under itself a second time, will be easier to untie after it has been under strain

Road trailers

The boat is pulled up the slipway on the launching trolley

Dinghies are frequently transported by road. They need to be securely supported in transit. Often a combination trailer is used. This has a launching trolley which is mounted and lashed on to the trailer itself. The trailer must of course conform to legal regulations for use on the road. The launching trolley is necessary because the heavy trailer is difficult to manoeuvre by hand and the wheel bearings cannot be put into the water for launching. On the other hand, if the boat is attached directly to the trailer, it is more secure on the road.

After the boat has been wheeled up the slipway, the mast is unstepped and the boat covers are fitted. The trolley can then be hauled on to the trailer and secured at the front and the rear. The halyards, stays and shrouds are lashed to the mast, and this too is secured. Last of all, the lights and number plate are attached at the back.

The cover is fitted over the top

Left: the under-cover is fitted to protect the hull from flying stones

Below: the trolley is bolted to the trailer at the front

On this type of trailer the boat is transported on its trolley. The mast is carried above

Double-decker trailers like this one can carry a second dinghy on top

Racing

Racing courses

Different designs of boat demand different types of course for racing. In the past the Olympic triangle was the favourite, starting with a beat to windward. More recently the International Sailing Federation has tested new course layouts which make it possible for several classes of boat to compete on one course, or to suit the specific characteristics of boat types, such as catamarans or windsurfers. There has also been a change in the number of *marks* (buoys) used in the course.

The aim is to avoid too much congestion at the marks, which must certainly have a favourable effect on the number of incidents between boats. A further change has been to sail several races on a single day of a regatta. There is, therefore, an advantage if the *committee boat*, from which the races are controlled, has not far to go to get from the finish of one race to the start of the next, so that little time is lost.

Problems at the leeward mark of an Olympic triangle

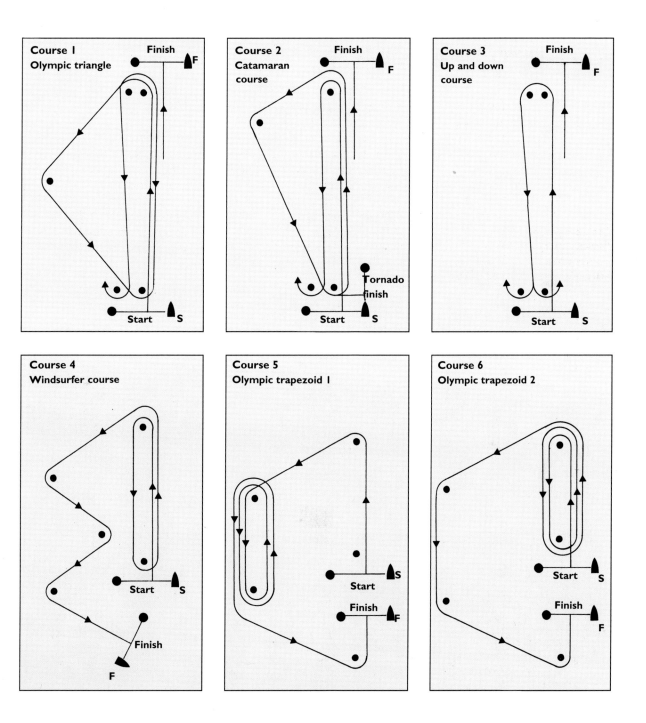

Course 1
Olympic triangle

Finish
F

Start
S

Course 2
Catamaran course

Finish
F

Tornado finish

Start
S

Course 3
Up and down course

Finish
F

Start
S

Course 4
Windsurfer course

Start
S

Finish
F

Course 5
Olympic trapezoid 1

Start
S

Finish
F

Course 6
Olympic trapezoid 2

Start
S

Finish
F

137

Dinghy classes

Sailing is a sport which appeals to very many different tastes. This is why there are so many *classes* (designs) of boat. Someone who prefers to sail alone may choose a different class from someone whose preference is for speed, or who wishes to compete in the Olympic Games. The singlehanded Europe dinghy is a good boat for lightweight men and women sailors, whilst the Tornado catamaran will suit sailors who like speed. The Laser also has a large following and so has the 420, a trapeze dinghy with spinnaker. The Contender, a singlehander with trapeze, or the Olympic two-man dinghy, the 470 (sailed by both men and women), are among the pinnacles of competitive dinghy sailing.

Top: the Europe, an Olympic class for women, is a singlehanded dinghy for the lighter helmsman

Middle: the 470, a two-man Olympic dinghy

Above: the Contender, an acrobatic singlehanded dinghy with a trapeze

The 420, a junior version of the 470, popular for racing and fun-sailing

The Tornado, an Olympic catamaran class

Sailing really does offer everyone a chance of finding a class suited to their body size and weight, and personal preferences. Another important influence on the choice of boat is the area in which it will be sailed.

The Laser, a highly popular singlehanded Olympic class

The Rules of the Road

One of two basic principles decides who has right of way when sailing boats meet, depending on whether both have their sails set on the same side or on different sides. It does not matter where the boat, or yacht, is coming from. What matters is the side over which the wind is coming to fill the sails. (Incidentally, it is not a question of rights, but of the duty to give way or to hold one's course. Even the boat which does not have to give way is still bound by the rules.)

Ever since the old days of sail when priority was accorded to the starboard tack, the yacht which is on port tack (has the wind coming over the port side) is the one which must give way. In Britain and the US the custom is for the boat on starboard tack to shout 'Starboard!', to draw the attention of the other boat to his obligation to take avoiding action. Other countries formulate the rule differently, but the principle is the same. Some think of the bow pointing to port, rather than the wind coming from starboard. They state this rule as 'Port bow before

starboard bow'. It comes to exactly the same thing as the rule that a boat on starboard tack has precedence.

If, however, both boats are on the same tack (have the wind on the same side), another rule comes into play. The yacht which must give way is the one which is to windward of the other. Sailors summarize this as 'Windward boat keeps clear'. If both boats are on exactly the same course, the one overtaking is obliged to keep clear.

Both these regulations are commonly spoken of as 'right of way' rules. There should be no problem as long as you remember that there is no such thing as a 'right' of way.

Above left to right: the windward boat must give way, even though the crew are busy hoisting the spinnaker. The other boat should keep a good lookout, but maintain a straight course

Below left to right: both boats are on port tack so it is the windward one which gives way, either by bearing away (as here) or by luffing on to a parallel course

Below: the boat close-hauled on starboard tack (right) has right of way over both port tack boats. The windward boat (left) must avoid both the others

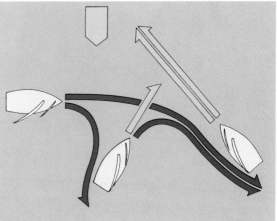

141

Clothing

To feel comfortable when sailing a dinghy, you need the right clothes. These should not be too heavy and should allow full freedom of movement. Comfort depends on the right combination of warm and waterproof clothing. The best waterproofs in the world will be of no use if one is steamed up inside in no time. So it makes sense to wear underwear which allows body moisture through and draws it away from the skin, as worn for other sports like skiing. Depending on the outside temperature, a thermal suit may come next. This is pleasant to wear and gives full freedom of movement. It is also easy to look after.

On top a one-piece suit is recommended for dinghy sailors as a protection against the wind and wet. The best choice is a suit with a waterproof zip at the front and braces (suspenders) worn inside, so you can take your arms out if the temperature rises. An inside pocket is useful.

The one-piece suits (right) have waterproof seals at the neck, wrists and ankles. The zip is at the front

Good protection against the cold is provided by this clothing. Over sports underwear the sailors are wearing two-piece thermal suits, allowing ease of movement

The braces (right) are extremely useful, enabling the top to be folded down on land or if conditions warm up

Another important detail (above); an inner pocket for personal effects

Safety equipment

Economies should never be made on safety equipment for any type of watersport. The dangers on the water cannot be stressed too much. One particular source of danger is water temperature, which is often low and leads to hypothermia more quickly than many people think. The correct clothing is therefore very important when sailing. It is advisable for dinghy sailors to wear waterproof suits, but they must ensure that trapped air cannot collect around their legs. This could have fatal consequences, because the buoyancy of the air may force the upper part of the body under water.

A lifejacket or buoyancy aid for every crew member is essential. A lifejacket will turn an unconscious person face up in the water, whereas a buoyancy aid will not. Nevertheless, many dinghy sailors prefer a waistcoat-type buoyancy aid because it is less bulky and easier to wear. The

Basic safety equipment includes a buoyancy aid for each person, a tow rope, paddles, knife, distress flares (or, as here, an emergency strobe light) and bailer

waistcoat also helps to keep the wearer warm. Automatically inflating lifejackets require more attention and will stay inflated after you have got up from a capsize, when you might rather they did not.

Other useful items would be flares to attract attention in an emergency. Standard equipment will include a tow rope, two paddles, a hand bailer (a scoop, bucket or similar to bail water out of the boat) and a sharp penknife.

If the dinghy is being used for cruising longer distances the following extras are needed: a first aid kit, a magnetic compass (with a means of mounting it on board), an anchor (a folding grapnel is most convenient) and a robust torch which will not fail the moment it comes into contact with water. A fog horn or aerosol signalling horn can have its uses at bridges or locks. Charts of rivers and lakes may also come in useful.

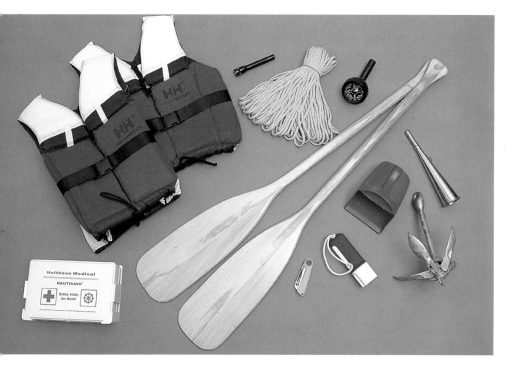

Additional safety equipment for trips further from immediate help includes first aid kit, compass, sound signal or horn, folding anchor and waterproof torch

Glossary

abeam in line with the beam of the boat (of something outside the boat)

aft towards the back of the boat

amidships in the middle of the boat, either relative to the ends or the sides

apparent wind the wind as it is actually felt on board, a combination of the true wind and the course and speed of the boat

astern behind the stern

athwartships across the boat from side to side

bail to empty water out of a boat or by hand

batten strip of wood or plastic inserted into a pocket to stiffen the mainsail

beam the middle of the boat on either side, the widest part

beam reach point of sailing when the wind is roughly at right-angles to the boat

bear away to change course away from the wind direction

beat to steer a zigzag course to reach a destination to windward

belay to fasten a rope to something

bend on to fit a sail to the boom or forestay

bilge bottom of the hull, inside or outside

block pulley

bollard short strong post used to secure ropes on the shore

boltrope rope sewn along the luff and foot of the mainsail to hold it into the groove in mast and boom

boom horizontal spar to which the foot of the mainsail is attached

bow the front end of the boat

broach to luff involuntarily across the wind when running before it, sometimes leading to a capsize

broad reach point of sailing between running and beam-reaching

bulkhead partition across the hull, which is often watertight

buoyancy tank watertight compartment which keeps the boat afloat after a capsize

burgee triangular flag at the masthead

cam cleat spring-loaded cleat consisting of two cams which secure a rope under tension

capsize (of a dinghy) to turn on its side

car moving part of a traveller, to which the sheet block is attached

catamaran or **cat** twin hulled sailing boat

centreboard vertical board projecting down through the bottom of a dinghy, which can be raised or lowered to counteract leeway when sailing

centreplate metal centreboard

chain plate metal plate on the hull to which the shrouds are attached

cleat device of wood, metal or plastic, used for securing ropes on the boat

clevis pin removable pin, which is secured by a split pin or ring, used to attach rigging etc

clew bottom rear corner of a sail

close-hauled point of sailing with the wind as nearly ahead as possible, as when beating

close reach point of sailing between close-hauled and beam reach

cockpit interior of a dinghy

crew second person on a two-person boat besides the helmsman

Cunningham hole in the luff of the mainsail, just above the tack, through which a line is passed to tension the forward part of the sail

daggerboard type of centreboard operated vertically, not pivoted

de-rig to dismantle the sails etc after sailing

dinghy open sailing boat with centreboard, as opposed to a boat with a fixed keel

displacement hull one which will not plane

ease release a rope in a controlled way

eye any of a number of types of rings, loops or circular holes

fairlead a guide for a sheet or rope, especially the jib sheet

fender cushioned object, usually made of inflated plastic, to protect the side of the boat from damage

foot bottom edge of a sail

fore-and-aft lengthways along the boat

foredeck the section of deck in front of the mast

forestay rigging wire supporting the mast from in front

free off to ease a sheet or rope and release it completely

freeing shift (freer) windshift causing the wind to come from less directly ahead

genoa large jib which overlaps the mast

go about another term for tack

gooseneck fitting for attaching the boom to the mast

goosewing to set the jib on the opposite side to the mainsail when running before the wind

GRP glass reinforced plastic (glassfibre)

gunwale top edge of the hull where it meets the sidedeck

gybe to turn the boat so the stern passes through the wind and the sails change sides

'gybe-oh!' warning given by the helmsman when he or she is tacking

halyard ropes or wires for hoisting sails

hank clip for attaching the luff of the jib to the forestay

head top corner of a sail, to which the halyard is attached

heading shift (header) windshift causing the wind to come from more directly ahead

head-to-wind pointing straight into the wind, therefore not sailing

head wind wind coming from straight ahead

heave-to method of holding the boat stationary (hove-to) with jib backed and tiller to leeward

heel (of a boat) to lean over at an angle

helmsman person controlling helm (tiller) and mainsheet in a two-man boat

hike out to use your weight out over the side of the boat to keep it upright

hoist to raise a sail or flag

hull body of the boat, excluding mast, rigging, sails etc

in irons or **in stays** caught stationary head-to-wind and unable to manoeuvre

International Sailing Federation worldwide sailing organization, founded in 1907 in London, to which the various national sailing associations today belong. Formerly the International Yacht Racing Union (IYRU)

jib triangular sail in front of the mast

keelboat boat with a fixed keel instead of a movable centreboard

kicking-strap rope or wire running diagonally between the front of the boom and the lower part of the mast to prevent the boom from lifting

launching trolley lightweight trailer for moving the boat in and out of the water by hand

lee helm tendency of a boat to bear away instead of continuing straight ahead if you let go of the tiller

'lee-oh!' warning given by the helmsman when he or she is tacking

lee shore shore to leeward of the boat which can be dangerous in strong winds

leech the rear or trailing edge of a sail

leeward the side furthest from the wind

leeway sideways drift or side-slip at an angle to the course steered, caused by the force of the wind

lift (of a sail) to flutter along the leading edge, indicating that you should pull the sheet in or bear away

luff forward or leading edge of a sail

luff (up) to change course towards the wind direction

mainsail triangular sail immediately behind the mast

mast gate channel to support the mast at the rear of the foredeck

mast rake slope of the mast away from the vertical

mast step fitting to hold the base of the mast. The position of the mast can often be adjusted fore or aft

masthead top of the mast

offshore (a wind) blowing from the land onto the sea

off the wind sailing on a reach or a run

onshore (a wind) blowing from the sea towards the land

on the wind sailing close-hauled or beating

outhaul rope for holding something out (eg the clew of the mainsail out along the boom)

painter rope attached to the front of the boat for holding on to it

pinch to sail close-hauled at such a narrow angle to the wind that the sails are fluttering and the boat is losing speed

plane to skim across the top of the water like a speedboat

point of sailing course relative to the wind (eg running, reaching, close-hauled)

port the left side, looking forwards in the boat

port tack any course with the wind on the port side and the mainsail to starboard

reach any point of sailing between running and close-hauled

'ready about!' preparatory warning given by the helmsman that he or she is going to tack shortly

reef to reduce the size of the mainsail

rig to get the boat ready for sailing

rigging collective term for all the wire and ropes of a sailing boat, especially the ones supporting the mast

rigging link length adjustment for shrouds and forestay by means of a plate bored with a series of holes

rigging screw or **bottle screw** length adjustment for shrouds and forestay by means of screw threads

roach convex area of sail created by the curve of the leech of the mainsail

roll side-to-side motion of a boat around its longitudinal axis, especially when running before the wind

roll-tack to roll a boat deliberately to windward before and after tacking to gain speed in light winds

Royal Yachting Association umbrella association of sailing clubs in UK, founded in 1875. National authority for sailing in Britain

rudder blade underwater section of a rudder, below the rudder stock or head

running before the wind sailing with the wind directly behind the boat

running rigging ropes and wires which are adjustable when sailing for controlling sails, mast and boom

self-bailer automatic device for removing water from the boat by suction

shackle bow-shaped metal fastening, closed with a pin (with or without a screw thread)

sheet rope used to control the angle of a sail

shroud rigging wire supporting the mast at either side

sidedeck strip of deck on either side of the cockpit on which the crew usually sit

sit out balance your weight over the side of the boat, without trapezing

spinnaker lightweight balloon-like sail hoisted on a reach or run

spinnaker guy the windward spinnaker sheet, controlling the pole

spinnaker pole light pole to hold the tack of the spinnaker to windward

splice to interweave strands of a rope to create a permanent join, either between two ends or to form an eye, instead of a knot

spreader horizontal strut attached half-way up the mast, so as to create a more effective angle of the shrouds

starboard the right side, looking forwards in the boat

starboard tack any course with the wind on the starboard side and the mainsail to port

stern the back end of the boat

surf (of a boat) to plane down the face of a wave

tack the bottom front corner of a sail

tack to turn the boat so the bow passes through the wind and the sails change sides

tang metal plate on the mast for attaching a shroud or stay

thimble rounded metal or plastic rein-forcement for an eye in wire or rope

thwart transverse seat in a dinghy

tiller horizontal handle used to turn the rudder

toe strap webbing strap along the inside of the cockpit for support when sitting out

track groove, in the mast or boom, for attaching the mainsail

trailer road trailer for towing a boat on land

transom flat stern section of the hull

transom flap hinged flap over an opening in the transom which can be opened to let water out after a capsize

trapeze wire secured near the top of the mast attached to a harness by which the crew can support his or her entire weight over the side

traveller slide carrying the lower block of the mainsheet, which can move along a track across the boat

trim the balance of the hull from bow to stern or from side to side, or the adjust-ment of a sail or sheet

uphaul rope attached to the mast, used to adjust the angle of the spinnaker pole

wake the disturbance in the water left by the passage of the boat

wash waves caused by passing vessels

way forward motion or momentum of the boat necessary for the rudder to have an effect

wear round or **wear ship** to avoid gybing by sailing round in a circle and tacking

weather another term for 'windward'

weather helm tendency of a boat to luff up instead of continuing straight ahead if you let go of the tiller

wheelbarrow turn manoeuvre to avoid gybing by sailing round in a circle and tacking

windshift change in wind direction. Can also be a change in apparent wind direc-tion caused by a gust or lull

windward the side nearest to the wind

Index

BRIDGWATER COLLEGE LIBRARY